CREATING A *Safe & Healthy*
HOME

By Linda Mason Hunter

Creative Publishing
international

CHANHASSEN, MINNESOTA
www.creativepub.com

Contents

Creative Publishing
international

Copyright © 2006
Text © Linda Mason Hunter 2006
Photos & step-by-step sequences
© Creative Publishing international,
   Inc. 2006
Creative Publishing international, Inc.
18705 Lake Drive East
Chanhassen, Minnesota 55317
1-800-328-3895
www.creativepub.com
All rights reserved

President/CEO: Ken Fund
Vice President/Publisher: Linda Ball
Vice President/Retail Sales: Kevin Haas

Cover Photo © Getdecorating.com

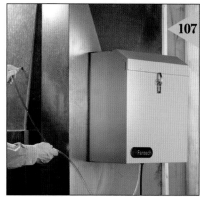

Executive Editor: Bryan Trandem
Creative Director: Tim Himsel
Editor: Andrew Karre
Art Director: Jon Simpson
Designer: Bill Nelson
Page Layout Artist: Joe Fahey
Photography: Andrea Rugg
Project Manager: Tracy Stanley
Photo Researcher: Julie Caruso
Production Manager: Laura Hokkanen

The Safe & Healthy Home
Library of Congress Cataloging-in-Publication Data

Hunter, Linda Mason.
  Creating a safe & healthy home / by Linda Mason Hunter.
      p. cm.
  Includes index.
  ISBN 1-58923-177-5 (soft cover)
  1. Home accidents–Prevention. 2. Dwellings–Maintenance and repair.
I. Title.
  TX150.H86 2006
  643'.028'9–dc22

843980123002-138

ACKNOWLEDGEMENTS

It took a small village to put together this book. My thanks goes out to everyone who helped.

A heartfelt thank-you to my editor, Andrew Karre, who stayed on top of every chapter to make it more in-depth, more informative, more up-to-date, and more useful.

Thanks, too, to my research assistant, Kelly Roberson, who slipped right in during a difficult time and eventually became my right hand, answering questions accurately, efficiently, and on time; to Scott Adam Johnson, a persistent and tireless researcher as well as a great help; and to architect Rob Whitehead for help and advice with the building and utility-related questions.

Thanks to my sources: Christi Graham, who helped me get started, Cheryl Luptowski at NSF International for reading over the water chapter and helping with accuracy, and Rick Andrew at NSF for last-minute help when help was needed. Thanks to Katy Hollbacher at the Green Resource Center in Berkeley, California, for her availability and for answering questions promptly; to Donald L. Lewis, professor of etymology at Iowa State University, who raised my consciousness about synthetic chemicals and toxicity; to Daryl Stanton, my main source for the furnishings chapter, and to her shop, Casa Natura in Santa Fe, New Mexico, a never-ending source of inspiration and beauty; to *Natural Home* magazine, where the article on Daryl Stanton and Casa Natura was first published; and to *HOME* magazine where the Safe, Healthy Remodeling chapter was first published. Thanks to Spark Burmaster, president of Environmental Options and all-around expert on electromagnetic radiation, and to John Banta for helping me understand the importance of EMR and the toxicity of mold.

And to my publisher, Creative Publishing international, for putting together all the helpful do-it-yourself projects so readers can actively create their own healthy environments.

Special thanks to all champions of creating a better world.

I dedicate this book to Scott, Ellie, Drew, Maxwell, children everywhere, and planet Earth.

About the Author:

Linda Mason Hunter is a pioneer in the healthy-home movement. Her 1989 book, *The Healthy Home: An Attic-To-Basement Guide to Toxin-Free Living*, was one of the first books on healthy homes written for the layperson. The New York Times called it, "a sort of *Whole Earth Catalog* for the home."

Hunter is also the author of *Southwest Style: A Home Lover's Guide To Architecture and Design, House Transformed: Getting the Home You Want with the House You Have* (with Matthew Schoenherr), and, most recently, *Green Clean: The Environmentally Sound Guide to Cleaning Your Home* (with Mikki Halpin). She is the founder of Healthy Home Designs and a founding member of GreenHome.com.

HEALTHY HOME UPDATE

We've come a long way in the last fifteen years. When my book *The Healthy Home: An Attic-To-Basement Guide To Toxin-Free Living* was first published in 1989, the U.S. Environmental Protection Agency had recently released a study that found levels of toxic pollutants five times higher inside our houses than outside. Back then, much of the knowledge and many of the products to remedy the problems did not exist. A revolution has occurred since then. Healthy alternatives are now available.

It's not all good news, unfortunately. Though awareness of the issues has become mainstream, the amount of pollution inside our houses is increasing. Over 85,000 synthetic chemicals are now in use. Manufacturers add more than 500 new chemicals to the mix each year. Most of these are not identified, let alone regulated. Complete toxicological data is available for only 7 percent of them, according to the Breast Cancer Fund, and more than 90 percent have never been tested for their effects on human health.

The Body Burden

These chemicals find their way into houses in building materials, furnishings, cleaners, and personal-care products. Most of these products are not reviewed before they come on the market, and manufacturers most often respond to consumer complaints only after a product is in wide use. No one knows the health consequences of exposure to a constant stream of these chemicals every day, especially when they act in combination with each other. But it is thought that every person on Earth is now contaminated. Scientific studies show our bodies may contain up to 200 synthetic chemicals, and a disturbing number of them are probable carcinogens. In addition, some are surprisingly similar in structure to natural hormones, and interfere with the chemical signaling systems within our bodies.

The human body is a marvelous organism. It can handle small amounts of poisons by excreting them (as it does with caffeine and alcohol, both of which are poisonous in high doses), but it begins to malfunction when overloaded with toxins. Toxic chemicals are stored in body fat, vital organs, the sheaths surrounding nerves, muscles, the brain, or spinal cord.

Surely it's not coincidental that the increased use of manufactured chemicals in the industrial world coincides with alarming health trends:

- One half of the world's cancers occur among people in industrialized countries, even though we are only one-fifth of the population. During our lifetimes, 40 percent of all Americans will get some form of cancer.
- Breast cancer rates are 30 times higher in the United States than in parts of Africa.
- Birth defects are on the rise, as are brain and nerve disorders like Parkinson's and multiple sclerosis.
- Sperm counts are declining, and there's a marked decrease in the number of male babies being born.
- The number of people with allergies is increasing. The rate among children in particular has doubled in the last three years.
- Disorders of the immune system are increasing at a rapid rate—15 percent of the U.S. population now suffers from chemical sensitivities. The National Academy of Science expects that number to rise to 60 percent by 2010.
- Asthma has reached epidemic proportions, afflicting 17 million people in the U.S.

In the U.S. today, chemicals are produced in such huge amounts that traces of them are routinely found in precipitation, sediment, and surface waters. A recent study is particularly disturbing. In 2003, the U.S. Geological Survey found low levels of household compounds in 139 targeted streams across the U.S., downstream from areas of intense urbanization. They include antibiotics, natural and synthetic hormones, detergents, antibacterial soap, caffeine, insect repellent, and an array of household cleaners. Of the ninety-five chemicals found (many of which are banned in Europe), drinking water standards have only been established for fourteen. Thirty-three are known or suspected to be hormonally active; forty-six are pharmaceutically active.

We're leaving a terrible legacy of poison and a diminished environment for our grandchildren and their grandchildren. How did things get so out of whack? It's a long story.

A Long, Strange Trip

Much of what we know as modern housekeeping has its roots in the Industrial Revolution. Throughout the 1800s, spring house cleaning was a confirmed American ritual—a weeklong marathon in which housekeepers and housewives whitewashed walls, aired mattresses, blacked stoves, beat the dust out of rugs, oiled woodwork, and painted rain barrels.

By 1913, the effects of the Industrial Revolution were clearly apparent. Changes in sanitation, agriculture, and general attitudes toward life led to a spectacular decline in mortality. Steel mills, auto plants, textile factories, railroads, and food processing plants brought employment, goods, and services closer to home. For the first time in history, motorized vehicles enabled people to travel with both speed and comfort.

Housing, too, reflected this change. Indoor plumbing replaced outdoor privies. Central heating replaced the wood or coal stove. Electricity lengthened productive hours of the day. The hand-cranked washing machine, icebox, and gas oven simplified everyday chores.

Still, turn-of-the-century "homekeeping" books stressed simplicity, economy, and thrift. *Household Discoveries and Mrs. Curtis's Cook Book,* a 1,200-page tome popular at the beginning of the 20th century, includes easy recipes for making soap, toothpaste, shampoo, cold cream, and toilet powder—all from readily available sources. Within its densely packed pages, a reader can find prudent advice on extinguishing fires, cleaning chimneys, disposing of household wastes, and eliminating flies.

Houses built in the early 20th century had some key advantages. Though solidly built, they were not tightly sealed, so air tended to pass through a structure fairly frequently. Most houses were sited to take advantage of prevailing breezes and the sun's light.

Then came World War II. Chemicals initially developed for the war effort found their way into America's houses—in cleaners, building materials, cosmetics, pesticides, and more. During the 1950s, advertisements promised to get clothes "whiter than white," make countertops "cleaner than clean," and bring "sparkle" to the toilet bowl. It was "better living through chemistry," as the slogan for DuPont sagely declared.

The 1960s witnessed another explosion of new chemicals in every type of consumer product. Synthetic fibers devised in the laboratory took the place of cotton, silk, and wool. Plastic replaced wood, glass, and metal. Styrofoam, instead of paper, became popular for drinking cups. Farmers sprayed chemical fertilizers and pesticides on the nation's farmlands to increase yields.

Though we weren't aware of it, America's houses were filling up with fumes from paints, stains, furniture, cleaners, and other human-made materials. To make matters worse, we were well on our way to becoming a "disposable society," one that encouraged buying a new "improved" item even when the one it replaced could be repaired.

The Fruits of Industrialization

By the 1970s, "sick buildings" became a part of the lexicon, a term coined to describe a building in which residents reported a range of adverse physical symptoms—lethargy and fatigue, headaches, dizziness, nausea, irritation of mucous membranes, sensitivity to odors, eye and nasal irritation, runny nose, nasal congestion, and general malaise. All were due to indoor air pollution, a result of poor design, bad ventilation, and a plethora of synthetic chemicals offgassed from furnishings, building materials, and cleansers.

In 1986, a five-year study by Harvard University scientists released by the U.S. Environmental Protection Agency (EPA) revealed that pollution inside the typical American home was two to five times worse than the grimiest outdoor air. A later study by the Consumer Product Safety Commission found that indoor air

Is Your House Making You Sick?

As much as we don't like to think about it, it's true that many of the products inside our own houses suppress our immune systems, leaving us more vulnerable to disease. In some cases, our houses are actively making us sick.

Medical problems caused by environmental hazards are far-reaching, ranging from respiratory irritations—stuffy nose, itchy throat, wheezing, shortness of breath—to more serious complaints of ear infection, asthma, and bronchitis. Such subtle symptoms as fatigue, headaches, inattentiveness, and dermatitis are possible reactions to an unhealthy environment. Many cancers, birth defects, and nervous disorders may be linked to environmental pollution.

Some people react more quickly to contaminants than others do. People who wear contact lenses, for example, often are bothered by environmental toxins in the air before anyone else is. People with allergies and respiratory problems may be the first to notice irritants. You needn't be diagnosed chemically sensitive to experience difficulties. For many, such ubiquitous phenomena as formaldehyde in carpeting and composite wood, hydrocarbons in vinyl furniture, perfumes, detergents, and fabric softeners cause severe problems. Some people have to make drastic adjustments—like removing all carpeting and pressed-wood products from their homes—in order to lead normal lives. Others make smaller adjustments—like avoiding gas heat and commercial soaps—in order to be comfortable. It's a matter of reducing the total toxicity to a manageable level so the immune system has a chance to recover.

It's a short road from good health to multiple chemical sensitivity. Many people become chemically sensitive to some degree after moving into a recently built house or shortly after completion of a remodeling. One theory about hypersensitivity is that the chemicals irritating hypersensitive people are poisonous to everyone—but most people never know it.

contained approximately 150 volatile organic compounds (VOCs), a type of airborne pollutant, while outdoor air contained fewer than ten on average.

In the United States today, you are most likely to breathe the most debilitating compounds at home. To make matters worse, we've insulated, caulked, and weatherstripped to the point where our houses no longer breathe; unsafe chemicals hang around inside for days, creating a potent synthetic brew.

The bottom line is that we are being exposed to thousands of synthetic chemicals that simply didn't exist in significant quantities on this planet until a few decades ago. The air inside our houses is so bad that the EPA continues to warn that indoor air pollution is a serious threat to human health.

Our unbridled consumerism is having its effect on the planet as well. In 2004, a World Wildlife Fund report stated that human beings consume 20 percent more natural resources than the Earth can produce. At this rate, by 2050 we will need the biological capacity of 2.3 Earths to maintain ourselves in the style to which we've become accustomed.

Is this how we want to live? It doesn't have to be. We can choose a better way of living based on diversified, renewable resources—a forward-thinking society that promotes health and well-being, both for ourselves and for planet Earth.

Multiple Chemical Sensitivity

Those dealing with diagnosed multiple chemical sensitivity (MCS) or environmental illness will certainly benefit from this book, but they'll want more thorough information on their specific sensitivities in order to create a home where they may be comfortable. For them, The Healthy House Institute is a good place to start. Another good source is the book *Prescriptions for a Healthy House* by Paula Baker-Laporte, Erica Elliot, and John Banta.

Chemicals Aren't the Only Danger

Chemicals aren't the only hazards in your home, of course. A modern house is in many ways a complicated "machine for living," full of clutter and intricate systems that can fail, with potentially disastrous results. From fires to falls and floods, there's no shortage of ways this machine can break down and harm your quality of life.

The Safe, Healthy Home

Do yourself a favor. Make your house a safe, healthy dwelling. You don't have to get rid of every synthetic molecule, just start down the path toward a more natural way of living. On a personal level, it will make you feel good. Your house will not only be clean and fresh, it will smell good and reward you in subtle ways. You'll unclutter your surroundings, making room for a new phase of life to unfold. You'll feel good about yourself, knowing you're doing your part to clean up the planet and make the world a better place for future generations. And you'll be helping your family lead healthier lives. You'll provide an example for others and learn a lot along the way. It may seem like a complex journey at first, but it is an attainable goal well worth the effort.

If you aren't currently chemically sensitive, you can compromise where you feel you must, but understand the human body is like a barrel. Toxins accumulate, a little here, a little there. Eventually, the barrel fills, creating toxic overload. Keep in mind that children are more vulnerable than adults. Because their bodies are smaller and their respiratory rates faster, they take in a higher percentage of toxins in proportion to their body weights. Pregnant women should be especially careful. Many of these toxins cross the placenta to contaminate the fetus.

The first step is commitment. This book shows you the way. Start by controlling the number of synthetic chemicals you bring into your house. Look for safer alternatives. Make compromises if you must. Remember, when it comes to harsh polluting chemicals, the lower the concentration, the lower the risk.

Cost should not be an obstacle. In many instances, the healthy answer is the simplest one, and therefore the least expensive. You'll soon discover you need less, and your life becomes simpler.

Think of your house as a third skin. If you nurture your physical body, keeping it tuned and healthy, you'll want to extend that TLC to your shelter, the four walls and roof surrounding you. It's an extension of yourself and your family. It deserves to be healthy, too.

In this day and age, achieving and maintaining a healthy home requires ecological awareness and a reconciliation between nature and technology. It takes mindfulness, every day, with every choice and decision you make. The way you choose to keep house, the everyday products you buy and use, the way you renovate and furnish, these daily decisions not only affect you and those who live with you, they affect the planet because of how products are typically manufactured and disposed of. Think about that each time you make a purchase.

Don't fall into the trap of expecting to change your whole house overnight. Getting a truly healthy, safe home is a gradual process, a series of little steps that requires time and thought. Like any commitment, transforming your house into a healthy, safe home comes with its own set of challenges. It takes awareness, education, and experimentation. As you become more successful, your house will become more comfortable. Along the way, you'll learn that quality of life has little to do with using harsh, polluting household chemicals. By its very action, achieving and maintaining a healthy home says there is a better way. Even the smallest changes make a big difference. So let's get started.

The Difference Between "Green" and "Healthy"

Green living is a philosophy that respects the planet's natural resources as well as human health. Most of the time, both "green" and "healthy" objectives can be accomplished simultaneously. Unfortunately, there are instances when the two schools of thought conflict. For this reason, it's important to make a clear distinction between the two so you can make wise decisions regarding your living environment.

Green living seeks to reduce the negative impact of a person's footprint upon the planet. Green building, for example, is focused on recycled materials, making use of waste products (such as recycled plastic lumber for decking) to reduce overall consumption. In addition, green building advocates use of technology to reduce waste, specifying engineered structural lumber, for example, instead of regular timber, thus reducing the need for old-growth lumber. Reducing energy consumption is important, so green builders incorporate passive solar and water conservation techniques.

Healthy living, on the other hand, focuses on human physical health, rather than overall environmental health. Particular attention is paid to using products that are safe, nontoxic, or chemical-free. Healthy design emphasizes pollution-free air and water. An example of a green product that is not healthy would be a carpet pad made of recycled tires. While this is an excellent idea from the perspective of reducing tires in the landfill, it is not a healthy product to use inside a home because tires continue to offgas during their lifetime, thus contributing to poor indoor air quality. Examples of healthy design that is also green include proper placement of windows and doors for natural heating and cooling, and use of natural lighting.

For the purposes of this book, healthy living includes a healthy planet, so green techniques and materials are always suggested when not in conflict with health criteria.

GIVE YOUR HOUSE
A HEALTH AUDIT

How safe and healthy is your house? Find out by giving it an audit, using the following checklist as a guide.

Since houses vary with age, design, building materials, and location, it's not feasible to cover all possible conditions. Houses built before 1980, for example, probably contain lead paint and may contain lead plumbing pipes and asbestos. New houses are more likely to have high levels of volatile organic compounds and other toxic chemicals. Flat-roofed houses are more likely to have moisture problems, especially if located in a rainy climate. Likewise, houses with crawl spaces may be more prone to mold problems than houses built slab-on-grade.

You may discover problems and concerns that do not appear on the checklist. Make a note of them and research them. Some items on this list may not apply to your house. Ignore them. The important thing is to be as thorough as possible in your inspection.

After completing the inspection, note the problem areas and list the repair and maintenance work the house needs.

Organize the list according to the severity of the problem, dealing with immediate problems before fixing cosmetic defects. Some problems must be fixed as soon as possible. These include the following:

- Conditions endangering the structure, such as a leaking roof, decaying structural supports, mold, or termite infestation.
- Fire hazards, such as faulty electrical wiring, worn insulation, or overloaded circuits.
- Hazards such as loose floor boards, weak railings, or decaying stair treads.
- Any problems that cause daily suffering, including objects that offgas, such as particleboard or new carpet.

Once you know the health problems in your specific dwelling, you can set about fixing them. Take care to solve the cause of the problem, not simply treat the symptom. Problems and hazards are dealt with in subsequent chapters, so reading the related chapter will help you prioritize your list.

Attic

Structure

❏ Framing and sheathing are solid and well-secured. Consult with a local building/housing inspector and/or structural engineer if you have questions.

❏ Areas around roof penetrations—chimney, plumbing vents, skylights, or long roof valleys— are dry and without evidence of leaks.

❏ The exterior soffit is solid and without signs of water damage or decay.

❏ Thermal insulation is present and dry. (Call your energy company to find out recommended insulation values for your area.) Insulation is not compacted.

❏ Ventilation or exhaust pipes that enter the attic continue on and out through the roof.

Ventilation

❏ Soffit and ridge vents or gable vents are present.

❏ All vents have bug and bird screens.

Safety

❏ A photoelectric smoke detector is installed.

❏ Flammable material is not stored in the attic.

Kitchen

Countertops

❏ All surfaces are hard and smooth with well-sealed joints to prevent moisture and food from getting trapped in the seams.

❏ Joints along the countertop and backsplash are well sealed.

❏ Seal around the sink is unbroken.

❏ Surfaces next to the oven or range are heat-resistant.

❏ Electrical receptacles are equipped with ground-fault circuit interrupters (GFCIs).

❏ Countertop appliances are unplugged when not in use.

Cabinets

❏ Cabinets are securely mounted to the wall.

❏ Cabinet shelves are solid and don't sag.

❏ Construction is of solid wood, metal, or exterior-grade plywood.

❏ Composite wood is properly sealed with a low-VOC sealer.

Flooring

❏ Flooring is resilient to prevent back or leg problems.

❏ Composite wood subflooring has been sealed to prevent formaldehyde offgassing.

❏ There is no vinyl flooring.

❏ Floor covering is a natural material, such as hardwood, true linoleum, cork, or bamboo, not vinyl or wall-to-wall carpeting.

❏ Flooring is nonslip and easy to clean.

Lighting

❏ A ceiling light provides overall room illumination.

❏ Work counters are lit directly from above, preferably with light from under a cabinet, cupboard, or shelf.

Major Appliances

❏ Refrigerator is an energy-efficient model.

❏ Gas range has spark ignition, not a pilot light.

❏ Flames of gas range are blue tipped, not yellow.

❏ Microwave oven door closes tightly.

Kitchen (continued)

❑ Countertop microwave oven has at least 24 inches of adjacent countertop.

❑ The oven is not a continuously cleaning or self-cleaning model.

Ventilation

❑ At least one operable window, preferably two, are present.

❑ Exhaust fan is present and is directly vented to the outside.

❑ The exhaust fan and filter are clean and free of grease.

Safety

❑ Photoelectric smoke detector and a fire extinguisher rated for grease fires are installed nearby.

❑ A carbon monoxide detector is present if the kitchen contains gas-fired appliances.

❑ A locked, ventilated cupboard for hazardous cleaning products is conveniently located in a kitchen pantry or laundry area.

❑ There are no commercial cleaners stored under the sink or in cabinets or drawers within reach of children or pets.

Cookware

❑ Cookware is glass, stainless steel, cast iron, or ceramic and does not contain Teflon or other synthetic nonstick coatings.

❑ Imported pottery with lead-based paint is used for decoration only.

❑ Drinking glasses are glass, not plastic or Styrofoam.

❑ Food storage and microwave dishes are glass, not plastic.

Dining Area

Flooring

❑ Composite wood subflooring has been properly sealed.

❑ Carpeting is not chemically treated.

❑ Floor finish is a natural material that can take spills without staining.

Table

❑ Table and chairs are sturdy, with no protruding nails or rough edges.

❑ Table and chairs are sized and situated to allow easy passage around them.

❑ Ceiling light hangs low over the table.

Living Areas

Ceilings
❑ Ceiling is not asbestos tiles.

Flooring
❑ Composite wood subflooring has been properly sealed.
❑ Flooring is a natural material.
❑ Rugs are untreated cotton or wool and have non-slip backings.
❑ Wall-to-wall carpet has not been treated with antistain coatings.

Furnishings
❑ Furniture is ergonomic, promoting a natural spinal curve.
❑ There are no particleboard furniture frames, plastic foam fillings, or synthetic upholsteries.
❑ Furniture is solid wood or metal, covered and stuffed with natural, untreated materials.
❑ Furniture is glued with nontoxic glue.

Lighting
❑ General room and individual task lighting are both sufficient.
❑ Artificial lighting is placed to minimize shadows.

Walls
❑ Paint is solid and smooth, not chipped, flaking or peeling.
❑ Walls are finished with an earthen material, plaster, or solid wood paneling.

Windows
❑ Window coverings are made of untreated natural materials.
❑ All windows have locks.
❑ After dry-cleaning, curtains and drapes are hung outside for six hours before being brought in.

Fireplaces
❑ Smoke or soot does not get into indoor air from fireplace fires.
❑ Chimney draws smoke from a lit newspaper within one minute.
❑ Damper closes tightly.
❑ Masonry is in good condition.
❑ Flue is lined and clean.
❑ The chimney has a rain cap.
❑ A carbon monoxide detector is located near the fireplace.

Safety
❑ A photoelectric smoke detector is present.
❑ Electrical cords are not run under rugs or carpets.

Bathroom

Structure
❏ Joints in wall coverings or along the floor are sealed.
❏ Caulking around the tub, shower, and sink is in good condition.
❏ Ceramic tile and grouting is solid without cracks or crumbling.

Flooring
❏ Floor covering is nonslip and easy to clean.
❏ Wall-to-wall carpeting is not present.

Cabinetry
❏ Cabinetry meets the same requirements as kitchen cabinetry.

Toilet
❏ Toilet is a water-saving model.

Tub/Shower
❏ A filter is installed on the showerhead.
❏ Showerhead minimizes water use.
❏ Watertight downlights provide general area lighting.
❏ Tub or shower is clean, with no sign of mold.
❏ Shower curtain is a natural material, preferably glass, hemp, or cotton duck, not plastic or any material treated for mildew resistance.

Ventilation
❏ Mechanical exhaust fan (rated at a minimum of 100cfm) is vented directly outside using the shortest route possible.
❏ An operable window is present.

Electricity
❏ Bathroom circuit is equipped with a GFCI receptacle.
❏ An adequate number of receptacles is present.

Safety
❏ A photoelectric smoke detector and a fire extinguisher are located near the bathroom.
❏ Tub or shower floor has rubber, nonskid mats.
❏ Rails are installed at the tub and toilet if elderly or disabled people live in the home.
❏ Medicine cabinet is out of reach of children or kept locked.
❏ Commercial cleaners are located elsewhere.
❏ Razors, soaps, and talc, are kept off the tub sides and out of reach in households with small children.
❏ Electric razors, blow-dryers, and curling irons are unplugged and put away after use.
❏ Towels are within arm's reach of the tub, and there is a minimum of 2 feet of towel rack per person.

Entryway

Flooring
❏ Flooring is sturdy and easy to clean and maintain.
❏ Composite wood flooring or subflooring has been properly sealed.

Lighting
❏ The entryway and door are well lit both inside and outside.

Safety
❏ A photoelectric smoke detector is located nearby.

Security
❏ Deadbolts or other secure locks are on all first-floor doors.
❏ Solid entry doors have a wide-angle peephole.

Stairs

Structure

❑ Stairs are structurally sound.

❑ Stairs, railings, and supports are sturdy.

❑ Framing around the stair opening is solid, without evidence of sagging.

❑ Stairs have 10-inch treads and 7-inch risers.

❑ Headroom is a minimum of 6 feet, 8 inches.

❑ A light, with a switch at both the top and bottom of the stairs, is present.

Safety

❑ Steps are clear; nothing is stored on stairs.

Adults' Bedroom

Structure

❑ Beds are situated away from walls abutting a high-energy-consumption appliance, such as a refrigerator or television set.

❑ Bedroom is wired separately so electricity can be shut off with a "kill switch" at night.

Flooring

❑ Carpet is untreated, and rugs have nonslip backing.

❑ Floor finish is a natural material without synthetic chemicals.

Bed

❑ Mattress is a combination of organic or green cotton, wool, and natural rubber latex, not synthetic materials.

❑ The mattress rests on open slats a foot or two above the floor.

❑ Pillows are filled with untreated natural material.

❑ Bedding is untreated cotton, wool, silk, hemp, or linen with organic cotton comforters, duvets, and blankets, not permanent press.

❑ The bed frame is solid wood glued with nontoxic glue, not metal or composite wood.

❑ Bed has at least 15 inches of standing space along both sides.

❑ Electric blankets or an electrically heated waterbed are not used.

❑ Clocks near the bed are battery-run or windup models.

❑ Television is more than eight feet from the bed if it must be in the bedroom at all.

❑ Electrical appliances are plugged in away from the head of the bed.

Closet

❑ Light is mounted at least 18 inches from clothing or other stored items.

Lighting

❑ The overhead light is operated with a switch right inside the door.

❑ A light switch or light is within reach of the bed.

Windows

❑ Curtains are an untreated, natural fabric.

❑ There are windows on two sides of the room.

❑ Each window has a lock.

Safety

❑ A photoelectric smoke detector and a carbon monoxide detector are located nearby.

❑ At least one window is operable and large enough to serve as an emergency exit.

Children's Bedrooms

Structure
❑ Beds are situated away from walls abutting appliances such as refrigerators or television sets.
❑ Bedrooms are wired separately so electricity can be shut off with a "kill switch" at night.

Flooring
❑ Flooring is natural, and carpets are untreated.

Furniture
❑ Furniture is solid, sturdy, smooth and constructed of wood with nontoxic glue.
❑ Babies and small children do not have pillows.
❑ Mattress is a combination of organic or green cotton, wool, and natural rubber latex, not synthetic material.
❑ Antique children's furniture and cribs meet current safety standards.

Lighting
❑ Artificial lights are inside sealed enclosures, like bulkhead lights.
❑ Sockets and receptacles are childproof.

Safety
❑ A photoelectric smoke detector and a carbon monoxide detector are located nearby.
❑ Track lighting is not used.
❑ At least one window is operable and large enough to serve as an emergency exit.

Electrical
❑ Cords are plugged in away from the bed.
❑ Clock near the bed is battery powered or windup.

Basement

Structure
❑ Foundation walls are solid with no signs of settling, such as large unaligned cracks in walls or inward-bowing walls.
❑ Wood in direct contact with soil or concrete is treated.
❑ Wood posts, sill plates, beams, or joists are solid, without signs of decay, water damage, or insect damage.

Moisture
❑ Walls and slab are solid without signs of dampness or efflorescence.
❑ Humidity is between 30 and 60 percent.
❑ Plumbing pipes are leak-free and don't sweat.
❑ Insulation is dry and uncompacted.
❑ Crawl space is well ventilated, mold-free, and has an effective soil vapor barrier.

Storage
❑ Paints or other flammables are stored in a UL-approved flammables cabinet.
❑ Tools are kept out of reach of children.

Ventilation
❑ Operable windows with cross ventilation are present in each room.

Safety
❑ Radon levels are below 4 picocuries per liter of air (pCi/l).
❑ Asbestos has been removed or encapsulated.
❑ A photoelectric smoke detector, a carbon monoxide detector, and a fire extinguisher are located here.
❑ Basement receptacles are protected with GFCIs.

Security
❑ All windows have bars and locks.
❑ Entry door or outside hatchway is equipped with locks.

Utilities

Electrical

❑ Extension cords are for temporary use only and do not run under carpets.

❑ Wiring has been checked and is adequate and up to date.

❑ There is no aluminum wiring.

❑ Surface wiring runs through metal conduit.

❑ Porcelain knob-and-tube wiring has been replaced.

❑ Circuits are clearly labeled at the service panel.

Heating

❑ Filters in a forced-air heating system are cleaned regularly.

❑ Gas-fueled appliances are sealed combustion and checked annually for leaks.

❑ Any gas-fueled appliance that is not sealed combustion has a reliable source of combustion air and is properly vented.

❑ Chimney is sound and is inspected annually.

❑ Furnace and other utilities are enclosed in a soundproof room.

Plumbing

❑ Supply line from city or well is copper, not lead or chlorinated polyvinyl chloride (CPVC).

❑ All supply piping is copper, not lead, galvanized iron, or CPVC.

❑ Pipes are soldered with lead-free solder.

❑ Water has been tested for lead contamination.

❑ Floor drain has been checked for sewer gas entering the house.

Garage

Structure

❑ Garage is detached.

❑ Attached garage is isolated from the house with a vapor-proof barrier.

❑ Attached garage is soundproofed.

Electricity

❑ All receptacles are GFCI protected.

Safety

❑ A fire extinguisher is located here.

❑ The electric garage door opener is set so that the door will immediately stop if an object crosses its path.

❑ All combustible materials are stored in a UL-approved storage locker.

Security

❑ Windows and doors are secure and lockable.

Yard

Electricity

❑ Lights are placed at the front, side, and rear of the house for security.

❑ Outside receptacles are GFCI protected.

❑ Yard is free of high-voltage power lines.

Gardens

❑ Lumber or timbers near food gardens are cedar and not wood treated with arsenic.

❑ Organic, not synthetic, pesticides and herbicides are used.

❑ Garden is mulched with untreated grass clippings.

❑ Yard is free of trash and overgrowth, particularly around the foundation.

Exterior

Foundation and Basement Walls
- ❑ House is level on its foundation, without signs of settling.
- ❑ Foundation wall is solid, without large open cracks.
- ❑ Masonry and mortar are in good condition.
- ❑ Ground is sloped away from the house for good perimeter drainage.
- ❑ Basement window wells are covered.
- ❑ Sill plates are free from rot and insect infestation.

Sidewalls
- ❑ Wood siding and trim is solid and in good condition.
- ❑ Siding joints are caulked.
- ❑ Window sills are solid, without signs of decay.
- ❑ Paint is smooth, not chipped, peeling, or blistered.
- ❑ Masonry and mortar are solid, without cracks or crumbling.
- ❑ Siding does not contain asbestos.
- ❑ Sidewalls are insulated.

Roof
- ❑ Roof is sloped with sufficient overhang to move water and snow away from the structure.
- ❑ Roof ridge is straight.
- ❑ Chimney is straight, and mortar is in good condition.
- ❑ Roof is not flat tar or gravel.
- ❑ Composition shingles are flat, well granuled, and asbestos-free.
- ❑ Wood shingles are solid, not ragged, rotting, or broken.
- ❑ Built-up roofing is supple, with no blisters or soft spots.
- ❑ Joints around chimneys, dormers, or plumbing vents or along valleys are well sealed.
- ❑ Roof flashing is continuous and tightly fitted.
- ❑ Eaves, ridge, and gable ends are vented.
- ❑ Gutters are well secured, clean, and slope properly to downspouts.

Doors
- ❑ Doors are solid, in good condition, and tight fitting.
- ❑ Exterior doors are weather-stripped.
- ❑ Joints around exterior door frames are caulked.
- ❑ Thresholds are solid and secure.
- ❑ Hardware is secure and operates smoothly.
- ❑ Doors have dead-bolt locks.

Windows
- ❑ Windows are weather-stripped.
- ❑ Caulking around window frames is solid and continuous.
- ❑ Window glass fits securely in the sashes.
- ❑ Glazing putty is smooth and supple.
- ❑ Wood frames are solid.
- ❑ All windows have security locks.

Porches
- ❑ Porch is solidly attached to the house.
- ❑ Stairs and railings are secure.
- ❑ Wood supports are on cement or stone footings, not in contact with the ground.
- ❑ Porch has a light.
- ❑ Wood in porches or decks is cedar, not creosote-treated or CCA pressure-treated.

Site
- ❑ There is negligible air and noise pollution from traffic and industry.
- ❑ Pesticide use in the neighborhood is minimal.
- ❑ Winter air pollution from neighboring fireplaces is minimal.
- ❑ The house is located away from high power lines, radio, TV, microwave, and cell phone towers.

WATER

Without water, there would be no life. The human body is one-half to four-fifths water, depending on percentage of body fat. Drinking enough clean water is crucial to good health.

In a healthy home, you want to ensure your tap water is as pure as possible. That's not easy these days. Every year, almost one million people in the United States get sick from contaminated water and 900 die from waterborne diseases, according to the U.S. Centers for Disease Control and Prevention.

Although the government has taken steps to protect water quality, there are a variety of pollutants present in tap water today, the inevitable result of a highly industrialized culture. They range from arsenic, to nitrates from fertilizers, to gasoline additives leaking from underground storage tanks, to volatile organic compounds (VOCs). In high enough concentrations, these pollutants can seriously harm human health.

In addition to industrial chemicals, aging pipes in cities throughout the country pose an imminent hazard to millions of people. In Atlanta, for example, pipes installed in 1875 make water so dirty it stains tubs, sinks, and toilets. The utility company purifies contaminated water with chlorine, but when too much chlorine interacts with dirty water, it creates toxic substances, such as chloroform, which has been linked to bladder cancer, miscarriages, and low birth weight.

Water utilities are required by law to monitor for 92 of the most harmful contaminants. But there are more than 2,800 chemicals in active use today, most of which are lightly regulated, if at all. No one really knows how dangerous these contaminants are or how they behave in the body. What is certain is that some of them are coming out of your tap. The good news is there are simple, effective steps you can take to protect your health and the health of your family.

What's In Your Tap Water?

Despite pollution controls on industrial discharges and sewage treatment plants, extensive water quality problems still plague our waterways. Recent studies show a broad range of chemical threats, most stemming from common products we use every day.

Some are regulated, meaning that water-treatment plants must test for them and assure the public that levels are below established maximum contaminant levels (MCL). But many compounds are not regulated, and thus they are not required to be removed from municipal water systems. The only way to know for sure if they are present in your tap water is to test it yourself.

Do your homework. Find out where your water comes from. Call your local utility or look at your last water bill. Be it lake, aquifer, or reservoir, visit the location and inspect the geography. Is any manufacturing going on around the water source? Is a large, pesticide-intensive farming operation nearby? Is it downriver from an urban area? See the Resources chapter (page 168) for information on how to find out what is contaminating the source of your drinking water. Then ask your water utility for a recent water quality report. From the EPA Web site, use the Safe Drinking Water Query Form to locate your water supplier and view its violations and enforcement history.

How to Read a Consumer Confidence Report

If you're on a public system serving more than 10,000 customers, your local water utility is required by law to include a contaminant report called the Consumer Confidence Report (CCR) with your bill by July 1 of every year. If you rent, check with your landlord. If you can't find the paper copy, check online at the EPA Web site.

The CCR explains where your tap water comes from, what EPA-regulated contaminants are in your local water and at what levels, and what needs to be removed. CCRs can be a bit difficult to read, so pay attention to the following items:

Regulated Substance List

These are the contaminants the EPA requires water-treatment plants to test for because they pose a health risk. Because the government compromises between health and economics when setting maxi-

mum contaminant levels, you need to think for yourself. If your CCR consistently reports a high level (anything near the maximum contaminate level shown on the CCR) of a certain substance—even though it meets the EPA standard for safety—to be safe, you may want to get a filter that removes or reduces it.

Violations

The CCR is required by law to include a list of all regulated contaminants that exceeded the EPA safety level in your system during the previous year. You may want to get a filter for these substances.

Lead and Copper

Because these substances mostly enter the water supply after water has left the treatment plant, you'll need to have an independent test done by a certified laboratory to be sure your water is lead- and copper-free.

Turbidity

If your water comes from a lake or river it will be tested for turbidity, or cloudiness. The higher the levels of turbidity, the greater the chance of disease-causing microorganisms being in the water.

Additional sources of information.

If you need help reading your report or want more information, call your water utility (the phone number will be on the CCR) or the EPA Safe Drinking Water Hotline at 800-426-4791.

Water Sources

How water gets to your house depends on whether you're on a public supply line or a private one. It's important to understand the differences and the role of government in each.

A public water supply is defined as any

system that regularly serves 25 people or more, including all city water supplies, rural water districts, and other supplies used by the public. Public water systems are controlled by state and federal drinking water regulations through the Safe Drinking Water Act, which requires routine monitoring and treatment of 92 contaminates to meet minimum quality standards. If the minimum standard for a contaminant is exceeded, officials must notify those served by that system. Depending on the level of contamination and the action required by consumers, notification may occur via television, radio, and newspapers—should the water present an immediate health threat—or through the mail in the next month's water bill.

The requirements fall short of ensuring that drinking water is free of contamination. Why? The number of contaminants monitored is small in comparison to the number that may be affecting drinking water. If a contaminant is not specifically tested for, it won't be found, even if it is present. Many of these contaminants cannot be removed by the treatment methods currently used. Requirements forcing a public water system to correct a contamination problem are sometimes loosely enforced, allowing continuous violation of some standards.

Private water supplies are all supplies not classified as public. Usually, these are wells used by one or two families and are the most common source of water for farms and residents of small towns. The quality of drinking water from private supplies is not controlled by state or federal regulations, nor are private supplies required to be treated or monitored. The responsibility for providing good quality drinking water lies with those who use it, so well water should be tested annually.

Experts contend that large municipal water systems, with full-time engineering staffs, are generally safer than smaller systems. But surveys show no link between the size of a utility and its water quality. As you can see, regulations provide limited protection to water users. Government agencies take only partial responsibility. The rest lies with you, the consumer.

Get It Tested

If you suspect an unregulated contaminant might be in your water, it's time to get a laboratory test. Testing for all possible contaminants is difficult and expensive, so you must choose which ones to test for. Your decision will depend on where you live, where your water comes from, what kind of contaminants you suspect may be affecting your water, and what the tests cost. If your water comes from a well, always request tests for bacteria and nitrates.

Many local water suppliers will test tap water for contaminants, sometimes without charge. There are also commercial water-testing laboratories. Choose a certified lab that uses EPA methods and quality controls, and whose sole business is water analysis. If they sell water-treatment devices, too, there is a conflict of interest. It helps if the lab you choose also offers consultation services to interpret test results.

After the lab has analyzed your water sample, you will receive a report of the test results, usually in parts per billion or parts per million. The lab will give you the federal safety standards so you can compare your levels and see whether your water meets those guidelines.

What You Can Do

After testing, you may learn that your

How to Test Water with At-Home Test Kits

Though there's no substitute for professional water testing and analysis, a variety of do-it-yourself kits are available to detect most common contaminates. The kits will give you a general idea of the types of contamination present in your water and can be helpful when choosing a filtration system.

Most test kits use special paper test strips to determine the levels of lead, bacteria, asbestos, nitrates, and other chemicals. Make sure to test cold water only, and carefully follow the directions for most accurate results.

drinking water contains one or more contaminants. Such a discovery can be unsettling, even if the level of contamination is within accepted "safe" limits. Of course, the lower the concentration, the lower the risk. If your drinking water contains contaminants, an in-home treatment device can help solve the problem.

In-home treatments fall into two categories—point of entry (POE) and point of use (POU). POE systems typically treat most of the water entering a home and are usually installed after the water meter. A water softener is a good example. Less expensive POU systems treat water at an individual tap. POU devices are available in countertop units (either manual fill or connected to a sink faucet), faucet mounts, plumbed in, plumbed into a separate tap, pour through, and pitchers. Refrigerator filters are also available to filter both drinking water and water used for making ice.

To guarantee your water treatment unit will perform as the manufacturer claims, look for certification or registration labels. Two private organizations, NSF International and the Water Quality Association (WQA), provide product testing (see page 168). While such certification is not necessarily a guarantee of safety, it is better than no certification at all.

Proper installation is the next step. Hire an experienced contractor or installer whose products conform to local plumbing codes. Be sure you understand how the system works; regular maintenance is critical and will likely be your responsibility. If not properly maintained, the system might make the problem worse.

In-Home Treatments

No single type of treatment can remove all water-quality problems. One or more technologies may be necessary to solve multiple problems. The following is a short summary of the types available. Before you choose a system, compare the contaminants listed as present in your water with the table at the end of this chapter (page 32). It will help you choose the most effective filter for your water system.

Filter Adsorption

Water passes through a filter media (usually in a cartridge), which either adsorbs or binds various contaminants. Common media include:

- **Granular activated carbon (GAC)** used for taste and odor control and to remove radon and organic compounds.
- **Solid block carbon** removes the same contaminants as GAC, but also removes lead, asbestos, some but not all forms of bacteria, and particulates.
- **Ceramic or synthetic fiber microfilters** removes various bacteria and particulates.
- **Activated alumina** removes fluoride, selenium, silica, and arsenic.

Reverse Osmosis

Water passes through a synthetic, semipermeable membrane that filters most pathogens and inorganic contaminants. If you incorporate a separate carbon filter into your system, the augmented reverse osmosis system can filter lighter pollutants such as formaldehyde, trichloroethylene, and other synthetic organics. It's a good idea to have a reverse osmosis system professionally installed.

Distillation

Distillers heat water in one chamber and turn it into steam. The steam then passes into another chamber where it is cooled and condensed to a liquid. Distillation can effectively remove microorganisms, dissolved minerals, metals, nitrates, and some organic contaminants. Distillation units require a dependable supply of electricity and usually produce only small amounts of drinking water.

Ion Exchange

Ion exchange systems are commonly known as water softeners. They replace calcium and magnesium (the minerals that make water "hard") with ions of sodium or potassium. Softeners can also be used to reduce iron and manganese and some radioactivity.

While softened water is better for laundering and bathing, the added burden of sodium in drinking water may cause health problems, especially for people who need to be on low-sodium diets. It's not difficult to treat your water so that you have softened water for washing and bathing but not for drinking and cooking. When you have a softener installed, ask that cold water taps that supply drinking water bypass the softener, or install a reverse osmosis device to remove the sodium.

Disinfection

The most common form of disinfection—which simply means killing harmful pathogens in water—is chlorination. Most public systems are required by law to disinfect their water, but individuals depending on well water must do this themselves. Ultraviolet light (UV) is a popular alternative disinfection technique because it doesn't use chemicals. UV is 99.9 percent effective if installed and used properly.

Aeration

Though aeration is a natural treatment in which water is exposed to air, it is typically suggested only for household use in rural areas where water is high in iron and manganese, thus making rust stains a problem in sinks, bathtubs, and toilet fixtures, and in the laundry where rust stains clothes. In such cases, an aeration unit is used in combination with a particulate fil-

How to Install a Point-of-Use Water Filter

Installing a water filter at a kitchen tap is easier than it sounds. Basic models install on the end of the faucet without any tools. For more comprehensive protection, multi-stage filters can be quickly and easily installed under a sink.

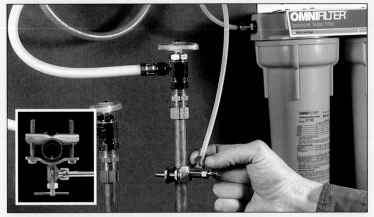

Mount the filter unit in a convenient location in the back of the sink cabinet. Turn off the water at the main shutoff valve. Use the saddle valve supplied with your filter to connect the filter to the cold-water supply pipe (inset). Clamp the valve on the pipe and tighten until the spike pierces the supply pipe. Connect the saddle valve outlet to the intake on the filter with the supplied vinyl-mesh tube and compression fittings. Don't overtighten the nuts.

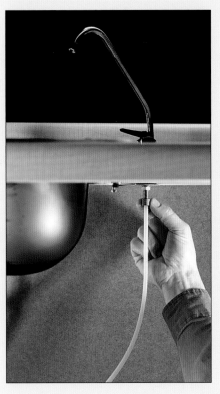

Install the filter's faucet unit on the countertop. Most models will fit in a sink's accessory hole (typically used for a sprayer). If there is no hole or it's in use, drill a hole in the countertop or sink deck as directed by the filter manufacturer. Set the faucet in the hole and tighten the mounting nuts. Connect the faucet to the filter unit with the supplied vinyl-mesh tube. Turn the water back on and carefully check for leaks. If there are leaks at the tube connections, carefully tighten the compression nuts until the leaks stop. Flush the filter as directed by the manufacturer.

ter. It is not needed in households on a municipal system because the water utility filters for iron and manganese.

Aeration is a POE installed in the basement or near where the main water pipe comes into the house. It takes the form of an open, vented tank in which air is pumped through water by means of a bubbler. Air is used as an oxidizer to change iron and manganese from soluble to insoluble forms, thus making the pollutants filterable. A pump then pushes aerated water through a sand filter or similar type of particulate filter that removes the insoluble iron and manganese oxides. Aeration units are expensive, take up a lot of space, and require professional installation.

Bottled

Bottled water is a popular alternative to tap water and may be an option if you can't treat your household supply, but bottled water is not necessarily safer than tap water. At least one-fourth of bottled water is actually tap water (some estimates go as high as 40 percent). Bottled water is regulated by the U.S. Food and Drug Administration (FDA), which has established water quality requirements similar to those established by the EPA for public water supplies. However, water distributed in the same state as its source is not required to follow FDA regulations.

If you choose to substitute bottled water for tap water, check with the bottler to find out where the water comes from and what minerals, chemicals, and bacteria may be in it; make sure the brand is certified. Look for the NSF International mark on the label or contact the NSF Consumer Affairs Office (see page 168). The safest containers for bottled water are glass.

Next best is polycarbonate, a durable, glass-like, nonporous plastic that doesn't leach into what's contained inside. If you want to carry a water bottle around with you, use a polycarbonate or stainless steel bottle (available at large health food and camping stores) and keep it clean.

Simple Treatments

If you're not ready to invest in a water purification system, there are some quick and easy remedies.

- Refrigerate water to improve the flavor.
- Allow water to stand several hours in an uncovered pitcher to dissipate heavy chlorine tastes and odors.
- Blend or mix water for 15 minutes with the lid off to aerate and remove chlorine and 90 percent of VOCs.
- Boil water for a few minutes to evaporate 90 percent of the VOCs.

Shower Filters

Though drinking contaminated water is one way for toxic chemicals to enter your body, showers and baths lead to even greater exposure through inhalation and skin absorption. During a ten-minute shower the human body can absorb 10 to 50 times the waterborne chemicals present in a single glass of the same water. The longer and hotter the shower, the more the chemicals build up in the air.

Removing chlorine is an important step, but removing chlorine byproducts (such as chloroform, chloramines, and tri-halomethanes) is even more important. Chlorine isn't listed on the EPA's list of carcinogens, but chlorine byproducts are. A dechlorinating shower filter removes chlorine and is easy to install, but to remove chlorine byproducts you need a carbon filter.

The next step up in shower safety is a filter that removes both chlorine and VOCs, a useful item since pesticides and other carcinogens and neurotoxins are increasingly present in our water. As a plus, the antibacterial capabilities of these combination filters often far exceed carbon shower filters.

Experts disagree on whether you should get a large filter that lasts a year or one with replaceable filters that have to be changed more often. If your water has high silt content, get a replaceable filter, or it will clog up in a short time. Some manufacturers contend a replaceable filter is the best option even in low-silt areas. Once you've decided on and installed a filter, remember to change filter cartridges regularly.

Common Contaminants

The following is a list of possible contaminants you are likely to see in high levels in tap water. This list will help you assess the risks involved if major contaminants are found in your drinking water and which in-home treatment devices will get rid of them.

Arsenic

Adsorption, Reverse Osmosis, Distillation

Arsenic, a naturally occurring mineral used in the manufacture of metals, glass, electronic components, and wood preservatives, contaminates the tap water of more than 34 million Americans. According to a 1999 study by the National Academy of Sciences, arsenic in drinking water causes bladder, lung, and skin cancer, and may cause kidney, prostate, and liver cancer. It also harms the nervous system and may cause birth defects, reproductive problems, and disorders of the immune and endocrine systems.

How to Install a Shower Filter

Toxins in water can enter your body through your skin, too. A shower filter is an inexpensive and easy-to-install way to protect yourself. Look for a model with multistage filtration to remove chlorine as well as VOCs and other synthetic contaminants. Always follow the manufacturer's guidelines for replacing the filter.

Remove your old showerhead from the supply pipe. You may be able to remove it by hand simply by turning it counterclockwise. If it won't turn, use channel-type pliers or an adjustable wrench.

Wrap the threads of the supply pipe with Teflon tape. Wrap clockwise so all the threads are covered with one layer of tape. Screw on the filtration unit. Hold the filter vertical and hand-tighten the nut. Flush the filter as directed by the manufacturer. If the filter leaks at the mounting nut, turn the nut carefully with a wrench or pliers until the leak stops.

Wrap the threads of the filter outlet with Teflon tape. Screw the showerhead onto the outlet and hand-tighten it. Depending on the filter model, you may use your old showerhead or one included with the filter. If the showerhead leaks at the outlet joint, tighten the showerhead carefully until the leak stops.

Hydrant Flushing

Watch your water bill for notice as to when fire hydrants in your area will be flushed. On that day, remove the filters from your treatment devices, as flushing can overload them with contaminants. Don't drink tap water on that day.

U.S. industries release thousands of pounds of arsenic into the environment every year. Until 2001, the EPA standard for arsenic in drinking water was 50 parts per billion (ppb), established in 1942. At that level, one in 100 people may get cancer—an extremely high risk. The current standard is 10 ppb, a level at which one in 500 people may get cancer—still a high risk. If the standard for arsenic were the same as for other carcinogens, it would be 0.5 ppb, a level at which one in 10,000 people may get cancer.

Asbestos
Reverse Osmosis, Adsorption

Asbestos is one of a small number of naturally occurring substances that are known carcinogens in humans. When found in water, it usually comes from asbestos-cement plumbing pipe installed after World War II. Though health risks from drinking asbestos-contaminated water are not known for certain, EPA studies show that where high levels of asbestos exist in drinking water, the cancer rate is above average.

The EPA can regulate asbestos levels in drinking water under the federal Clean Water Act, but few towns or cities can afford to replace entire water supply systems, so high levels often go untreated.

Bacteria
Chlorination, Reverse Osmosis, Ultraviolet Disinfection

Despite the publicity surrounding synthetic chemicals, bacterial contamination remains the most common water-quality problem in individual and small systems. Contaminating organisms commonly originate in human and animal wastes and find their way into groundwater from improper septic tank drainage, sewage, feedlot manure, or direct drainage of surface runoff into a well. Drinking water contaminated with bacteria can result in a variety of infectious diseases, including dysentery, cholera, hepatitis, and typhoid fever. If you have a private well, have it tested periodically for coliforms, cryptosporidium, e.coli, and giardia lamblia.

Public water systems use a variety of additives to kill bacteria before it reaches the public. But aging pipes (a problem in most cities) are prone to bacterial contamination when pumps fail or a water main breaks.

Individual household systems can also become contaminated by back-siphoning, which occurs when standing water flows backward into a system through faucets or hoses (this can happen when a garden hose is left lying on the ground in a puddle). Prevent this from happening by installing antisiphon devices on hoses and make sure irrigation systems are properly installed.

Lead
Adsorption (carbon/charcoal), Reverse Osmosis, Distillation

According to EPA estimates, 20 percent of human exposure to lead is through drinking water. Old plumbing pipes, lead-based solder, and brass-alloy faucets are the major causes of lead contamination in household water. Although federal standards limit the amount of lead in water to 15 ppb, independent research makes a strong case for a limit of 10 ppb or less. If tests show that the level of lead in your household water is at this point or higher, it is advisable (especially if there are young children in the home) to reduce the lead level in your tap water as much as possible. Health effects include kidney and nervous system damage, learning disabilities, adverse behavioral changes, seizures, coma, and death. Children and pregnant women are particularly susceptible.

Many companies offer home test kids for lead, generally from $10 to $25 at hardware stores, home centers, and on the Internet, but the EPA, the Water Quality Association, and other groups recommend professional testing, usually costing about $100, by a certified laboratory for reliable results.

If you decide the risk in your home is so low it's not worth testing, you can still reduce lead exposure. Because water standing in pipes tends to absorb lead, always flush the pipes before drinking by letting your tap run until the water is cold. This must be done with each faucet before you drink water from it. Also, never use water from the hot tap for drinking, cooking, or making baby formula, as heat increases the corrosion of lead.

Metals
Reverse Osmosis, Distillation, Adsorption (carbon/charcoal) for some but not all

Soft metals—such as aluminum, copper, chromium, and lead—can be found in trace amounts in drinking water and can accumulate over time in human tissue, causing liver, brain, and kidney damage. Aluminum is linked to Alzheimer's disease. In a recent French study, scientists determined that a concentration of aluminum in drinking water above 0.1 mpl (milligrams per liter) may be a risk factor of dementia and Alzheimer's disease. Aluminum is not regulated, but the EPA recommends no more than 0.2 ppm. For copper and chromium, 0.1 ppm is the maximum. For lead, acceptable levels are less than 15 ppb. Most municipal water utilities are required by the state to treat water or find an alternate water source when excessive levels of metals are detected in the water supply. For those relying on well water, each well must be tested individually since two wells separated by a few hundred feet can have very different metal levels.

Nitrates
Reverse Osmosis

Nitrates enter the water through feedlot wastes, failed septic systems, landfills, and garbage dumps, but by far the main source of contamination is through nitrogen fertilizer runoff. Nitrates from lawn or garden fertilizer can also be introduced into any system by backsiphoning through a garden hose. Nitrate contamination is particularly serious in Midwestern states that rely on agriculture as a main industry, and in California where nitrates are the major polluter of groundwater. Studies conflict on the health effects of nitrates, but there is reason to suspect they cause non-Hodgkins lymphoma and other cancers.

Municipal water systems regularly test and filter for nitrates in water, but private wells and many community wells serving fewer than 25 people may not. For them,

dealing with elevated nitrates in water is difficult. Nitrate levels tend to fluctuate depending on the time of year, so tests need to be taken periodically. Boiling is not effective, and filtering is expensive. Once a well-water system is contaminated with nitrates, drilling a new well is usually the only realistic alternative.

Pesticides
Adsorption (carbon/charcoal)

Municipal water systems are required to test for pesticides and to provide treatment or alternate supply sources if problems arise. If you live in an area where industrial farming uses large amounts of chemical pesticides, it's a good idea to get a carbon filter to treat water in the entire house. Be sure to change the filters in the spring and be sure they are effective during periods of heavy rainfall.

For those using well water, be extremely cautious about using pesticides and other chemicals on your property. Never use or mix a pesticide near the wellhead. The well should be tightly sealed and extend downward to aquifers that are below, and isolated from, surface aquifers. To get information on your well, you can call the contractor who installed it, or check code in your area.

If your well water is analyzed and found to contain pesticide residue levels above recommended health standards, use an alternate water source, such as bottled water, for drinking and cooking. A water filter can provide some peace of mind, but if pesticide levels are high, a filter will probably not remove all of them.

Perfluorochemicals
Adsorption (granulated activated carbon)

The reliance of U.S. consumers on perfluorochemicals (PFCs) is contaminating

How to Install Vacuum Breakers & Air Gaps on Faucets & Dishwashers

Contaminated water from the yard or from a backed-up washing machine or dishwasher drain can mix with drinking water and poison you. Vacuum breakers on faucets and air gaps on dishwashers prevent wastewater from backing up into drinking water.

Confirm that all outdoor faucets have vacuum breakers. If they don't, install inexpensive screw-on vacuum breakers, available at hardware stores and home centers.

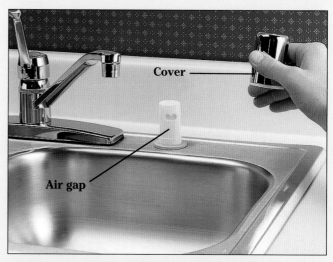

Make sure your dishwasher has a properly installed air gap. Installers sometimes skip the air gap. Most models have an air gap installed on the top of the sink. If your dishwasher doesn't have an air gap, call a plumber to install one.

air and water all over the world. Researchers have even found PFCs in the blood of arctic wildlife. These are a new class of human-made chemical used in heat- and water-resistant products, from clothing and carpets to cookware, computers, cosmetics, household cleaners, and fast food packaging. They can travel great distances, are extraordinarily resistant to breaking down, and persist in the environment for years. PFOA (perfluorooctanoic acid, a type of PFC used in Teflon) is found in the blood of 95 percent of Americans.

A flood of disturbing scientific findings since the late 1990s has abruptly elevated PFCs to the rogues' gallery of highly toxic, extraordinarily persistent chemicals that add to the human body burden. Though more studies need to be done, low levels of PFCs are suspected of causing a wide range of tumors on the rise in America today, including breast, testicular, liver, and prostate. They are also linked to developmental problems and high cholesterol, a risk factor for heart attack and stroke. PFOA is currently the subject of a federal investigation and three class-action lawsuits.

Recent studies show extremely high levels of PFCs contaminating drinking water supplies near manufacturing plants in six eastern cities. But they are surely present in other locations, as well, particularly around manufacturing plants. Since PFCs are not on the EPA list of regulated contaminants, water-treatment plants are not required to test for them. Though maximum contaminant levels have not been

Water Filter Types

Type of Unit	Contaminants Removed	Upside	Downside	Installation
Carafe A pitcher with an activated-carbon filter. Brita is a popular carafe-type water filter.	Bad tastes & odors, benzene, chlorine, chloroform, lead, mercury, sediment	• Low-cost. • No plumbing work required.	Filter must be changed often to maintain effectiveness.	None required.
Faucet mounted Faucet-attached activated-carbon filter.	Bad tastes and odors, benzene, chlorine, chloroform, cysts, lead, mercury, some pesticides, sediment	• Easy installation. • Dispenses filtered water straight from the tap.	Filter cartridges need to be changed often to prevent clogging.	Do it yourself.
Under the sink Activated-carbon filter fitted to pipes attached to the faucet.	Bad tastes and odors, benzene, chlorine, chloroform, cysts, lead, mercury, some pesticides, sediment, VOCs	• Water flows quickly. • Doesn't clog quickly.	Takes up space under the sink.	Do it yourself.
Reverse osmosis Water is pushed through a membrane that filters contaminants.	Arsenic, bad tastes, calcium, chlorine, chloroform, dissolved solids, fluoride, lead, mercury, nitrates, sediment, sodium	• A good all-around filter, especially when used in combination with a carbon filter.	Expensive filter needs replacement once a year.	Call a plumber to install.
Whole-house system Filters installed at the household water main. Can be carbon, reverse osmosis, or other type.	Depends on the type of filter.	• Can be individually designed to remove the specific contaminants in your system. • A good first filter.	May require point-of-use filters, as well.	Call a plumber to install.

set, some states have established health-based values (HBV). Different types of PFCs have different HBVs, and HBVs differ from state to state. For example, in Minnesota, the HBV for PFOS (perfluorooctane sulfonate) is 1 part per billion (ppb). The HBV for PFOA is 7 ppb.

If you suspect PFCs may be contaminating your drinking water, have a sample tested for PFC levels. If you find even trace amounts, it's a good idea to get a granulated-activated carbon filter installed as part of a whole house filtration system or, at minimum, install one at the kitchen tap.

Radon
Adsorption, Aeration

If you live in an area with elevated levels of radon, it is possible for radioactive gas to contaminate household water. Individual wells and small-town systems present the greatest concern; water from municipal systems releases most of its radon before it reaches individual houses.

Since radon is more likely to affect people through the air they breathe, the main cause of concern comes from activities such as showering, bathing, and washing. If you suspect radon may be in your water, have it tested. Radon detectors are available for those on a well system.

If levels higher than 300 picocuries of radon per liter of water (pCi/L) are found, consider purchasing radon-removal equipment to treat the entire household water supply.

Trihalomethanes
Adsorption (carbon/charcoal)

When chlorine is added to municipal water systems to kill bacteria and reacts with organic matter, such as rotted leaves, methane gas is given off and forms trihalomethanes, or THMs, which are linked to cancers and reproductive problems. When it comes to THMs, showers pose as much, or more, of a problem as drinking contaminated water does. Researchers at the CDC report that THM levels in women's blood quadrupled after they showered.

Levels of THMs in small-town water systems are often higher than the federal standard of 80 ppb. In city systems, the longer the water sits in a pipe, the higher the THM content may be. If you're at the tail end of a city plumbing system, water coming out of your faucet is likely to carry a higher level of THMs than water closer to the treatment plant.

Volatile Organic Compounds
Adsorption (carbon/charcoal)

All organic substances contain carbon in combination with other elements, such as oxygen or hydrogen. They include pesticides, trihalomethanes, and petroleum products, in addition to others. The concentration of organic chemicals in drinking water is usually too low to produce acute toxic effects, so chronic toxicity is the main concern. Residents of communities where water has been contaminated by VOCs suffer a range of health effects, from skin rashes and terminal illnesses, to high rates of miscarriages and birth defects.

Public systems are required to test for only a small fraction of VOCs. The only way to find out for certain if they are present in your drinking water is to test, which is more expensive than tests for other contaminants.

A Healthy Home Has…

- A water-treatment system certified to address the impurities of city-supplied or well water.

- A shower filter to eliminate chlorine, chlorine byproducts, and other impurities.

- A refrigerator water filter for refrigerators with automatic ice makers or water dispensers.

INDOOR AIR

The U.S. Environmental Protection Agency continues to warn that indoor air pollution is a serious threat to human health. Indoor air is two to five times more polluted than outdoor air, and is among the top five environmental risks to public health.

Two types of indoor air pollutants affect human health: biological and chemical. Common sources of biological pollutants are humidifiers, air conditioners, mattresses, pets, and carpets. Common sources of chemical contaminants include oil and gas appliances, tobacco smoke, paints, pesticides, and many household products.

When it comes to indoor air pollution, climate has a marked effect. High heat levels release toxic vapors in paints, metals, and building materials. High humidity accelerates the release of formaldehyde and other VOCs. Fumes capable of causing a multitude of subtle physical and mental symptoms are released at low, or even normal room temperatures.

Is your indoor air polluted? Do you notice any smells? Has anyone commented on the smell in your house? It could be anything—last night's dinner, stale tobacco smoke, musty smells from mold and mildew, gaseous odors from combustion appliances, a noticeably chemical odor, fragrance, car exhaust, or smells coming from a home office—copy paper, printer, copy machine. Anything you smell you are breathing into your body. Try to locate the source of any noticeable smell

Effects of Indoor Air Pollution

Indoor air pollution may be to blame for any of the following:
- Headaches, fatigue, shortness of breath
- Sinus congestion, coughing, sneezing
- Eye, nose, throat, and skin irritation
- Dizziness, nausea

If you or someone in your family is experiencing these symptoms, check for the source of pollution in the order of immediate hazard: combustion byproducts and carbon monoxide, mold, bacteria and viruses, lead paint, volatile organic compounds (particularly formaldehyde), allergens, second-hand tobacco smoke, or electromagnetic radiation.

and eliminate it. Don't mask the smell with air freshener or other perfume. This simply introduces more chemicals into the air.

Top Ten Polluters

Because not all pollutants have smells, it's important to know what may be in the air you're breathing. The following is a synopsis of the ten most common indoor air polluters.

Volatile Organic Compounds

By definition, volatile organic compounds (VOCs) are carbon-based chemicals that form vapors at room temperature. Primary organic compounds are derived directly from natural gas, oil, and coal, including propane, butane, benzene, xylene, paraffins, and toluene. These, in turn, are used to make intermediate substances like formaldehyde, phenols, acetone, isopropanol, and acetaldehyde—substances used in a host of household products.

You're likely to encounter VOCs almost anywhere in a house. They're found in plywood, particleboard, wood paneling, carpets, carpet pads, insulation, paints and varnishes, solvents, adhesives, synthetic fabrics, detergents, waxes, body-care products, mothballs, insecticides, aerosols, art and hobby materials, dry-cleaned garments, and (ironically) air fresheners.

The "volatile" in VOC means they offgas into the air, contributing to air pollution. Some substances offgas most of the VOCs they contain in a short period of time. Paint, for example, offgasses 80 to 90 percent of its VOCs within a couple of weeks of application; the remaining 10 to 20 percent offgas over the next year, mostly during times of higher temperature and humidity. Adhesives and insulation that contain formaldehyde, on the other hand, offgas very slowly, sometimes over years, depending on temperature and humidity.

Formaldehyde (a suspected carcinogen) is so common that some experts believe it to be the single most pervasive indoor air pollutant. Formaldehyde is found in building materials, floor coverings, paint preservatives, insulation, furniture, textiles, mattresses, and a wide variety of personal care products, including toothpaste. Formaldehyde is linked to brain and other cancers, leukemia, liver damage, nervous ailments, and breathing disorders.

Common symptoms of VOC exposure include minor eye, nose, and throat irritation; shortness of breath; headaches; nausea; and lethargy. Though you won't die from breathing the fumes, quality of life is definitely diminished. Air fresheners and aerosols, for example, are known to harm babies both before birth and in early childhood. Recent Australian studies found a link between VOCs and childhood asthma.

Prevent VOCs from contaminating the indoor air simply by not introducing them in the first place. There are non-VOC paints, for example, as well as low-VOC alternatives for all building materials. Usually, the more natural the composition, the better. If you already have products containing VOCs in your house, there are ways to limit the problem. Sealing composite wood with a sealant that prevents further offgassing, for example, prevents formaldehyde from getting into the air. See pages 50 to 51 for more on sealants.

Tobacco Smoke

During any five-year period, more Americans die from smoking than from all the wars the United States has ever fought. And you don't have to be a smoker to feel the effects of smoke. If you live in an apartment or condo where smokers live, you may have smoke in your living space. If you purchased a home from a smoker, smoke may still pollute the air. Once smoke pollutes indoor air, odors cling to walls, furnishings, draperies, clothing, and other materials where it is released slowly for days, weeks, and years. Even where there is good ventilation, odors may persist and contaminate the air.

Tobacco smoke not only harms the smoker, it's bad for anyone who breathes the smoke-polluted air. The most irritating smoke comes directly from the burning end of the cigarette. This side-stream smoke has higher concentrations of noxious compounds than smoke inhaled by the smoker. Children are especially at risk due to their size and higher respiration rates.

Mold

Mold is found everywhere—indoors or out. When mold-spore counts are higher indoors than outdoors, it signifies a problem with moisture in the building. Mold can grow anywhere it has sufficient moisture and a food source. Its spores settle on surfaces and can infiltrate ductwork. An even bigger health problem than visible mold is a chemical byproduct, called mycotoxins, some types of fungi leave behind when they die. There is evidence that mycotoxins cause cancer and neurological damage and suppress the immune system.

Over time, people become less tolerant of mold. An allergy to mold often leads to other allergies. Some molds (like stachybotrys, penicillium, and aspergillum) spawn more health problems than others. Some are potentially toxic and, with time, can kill.

Moisture from leaks is a frequent cause of mold. It's common for water to leak slowly

How to Test for Mold

Home testing for mold is, at best, an inexact science. Though inexpensive kits are abundant, interpreting results isn't always straightforward. For the most accurate results, professional sampling and evaluation are in order. Professionals will take indoor and outdoor samples to establish base levels of environmental mold. Mold-abatement specialists can usually be found in the phone book.

Home test kits that have you take the sample and send it to a lab for evaluation are a good second-best choice. If you suspect mold, test areas like basements, bathrooms, attics, and crawl spaces. If results show mold infestation, call a mold specialist for comprehensive testing and abatement.

Unpack the test strips as directed by the manufacturer. Lightly press the sticky side of the test strip to a surface where you suspect mold growth. Peel back the strip. Don't overload the strip by pressing too hard. There should be some material on the strip, but the strip shouldn't be entirely covered.

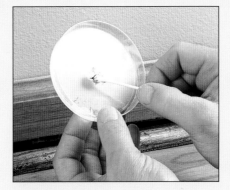

Place the strip on a plastic slide attached to the mailing card, and label the strip with the room and surface you sampled. Repeat the first two steps for any other rooms where you suspect mold growth.

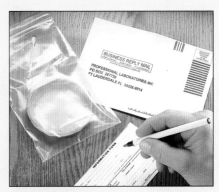

Mail the strip back to the testing company. Reputable testing companies will provide clear results in a couple weeks.

into wall cavities from small plumbing leaks, sweating pipes, or poorly sealed openings for years before the problem is detected. Make sure all openings in the building envelope are correctly sealed so water doesn't leak into the walls and roof. Check around all plumbing fixtures for leaks, and correct them immediately.

Most molds thrive in low-light conditions, so providing lots of light and an uncluttered environment is also a good preventative.

Mold is also commonly found in poorly ventilated bathrooms and cluttered basements, especially if you have piles of newspapers or magazines stored in a damp corner. Crawl spaces are another frequent site of mold contamination. If you have a crawl space underneath your house, see that it is ventilated all year-round. Cover the ground and floor joists above the crawl space with a poly barrier to keep mold spores from entering the air.

Remediating a building when mold is found requires sealing off the contaminated area, cleaning up or replacing all mold-infested surfaces (including drywall, ceiling tiles, and flooring materials), and then fixing the cause of leaks that allowed moisture to get in.

Bacteria & Viruses

Airborne bacteria and viruses carry infectious diseases such as influenza, tuberculosis, measles, chicken pox, and rubella. Most are transmitted by people through coughing, sneezing, and breathing. However, a complex mixture of amoebas, bacteria, molds, and fungi breed in water reservoirs in humidifiers, air conditioners, and vaporizers. When improperly maintained, these appliances provide an ideal environment for breeding and dispensing tiny microbes.

Freestanding humidifiers are the worst culprits. When in use, they must be regularly emptied, cleaned, and refilled with clean water. Vaporizers are common culprits, too. When using one, put hot water in to begin; never allow water to stand for long periods of time; and empty, clean, and disinfect the unit with hot water and vinegar at least once a day.

Heating and air conditioning systems can breed and disperse bacteria and viruses, as well. Keep these units well maintained and cleaned. Be sure the air conditioner drain pipe is always dripping water when the air conditioner is on. If it's not, the drain could be backed up, meaning there's a good chance of standing water in the system. If you have a window unit, make sure it is tilted so it drains properly.

If your house has forced air heating and cooling, hire a professional to clean the air ducts periodically. Follow good ventilation practices (see page 112). Frequently air out your home.

Allergens & Asthma Triggers

Asthma and allergies can be life-threatening conditions. People with allergies or asthma are sensitive to "triggers," including particles in the air. These "triggers" can set off a reaction in the lungs as well as other parts of the body. Since people spend more than 20 hours per day indoors, it's important to identify the substances that are causing problems, then take remedial efforts to get rid of them. Here's a list of some of the most common allergy triggers.

Dust Mites

Though you can't see them, dust mites are the single most common allergen found in houses. Colonies thrive at 70 percent humidity, so they tend to hit their peak in late summer. Mites proliferate in climates where winters are humid and mild. Since humidity decreases with increasing height above sea level, mites are less common at high altitudes.

Mite count is almost always highest in the bedroom. Air it out! Open bedroom windows whenever possible to reduce dust and other air pollutants. Open windows at least a little bit every day, if your climate allows. Hang blankets and comforters on the clothesline in the sun for three or four hours to air them out. This

Natural Air Cleaners

House plants are used to clean indoor air naturally. Those known to soak up air pollutants include chrysanthemums, dracaena palms, philodendrons, schveffleras, spider plants, English ivy, and bamboo. To appease allergies, place a layer of aquarium gravel atop plant soil. To prevent mold, do not allow plants to stand in water.

kills microorganisms and keeps bedclothes smelling fresh. Air out mattresses a couple of times a year to kill mites and discourage mold and funguses. Pillows need to be aired and sunned more often. Don't put bedding outside on high pollen count days. If you live in a city and airing out is impossible, be sure to launder mattress pads and linens in hot water, and vacuum pillows and mattresses.

Mites are found in upholstered furniture, as well. Avoid upholstery with deep, sculpted fabric. Hardwood and cane furniture are best. For covered furniture, naturally tanned, undyed leather, is a good choice.

Pollen

Contact your county cooperative extension office, and find out when plants you're allergic to typically pollinate your area. Pay attention to pollen reports, and limit your time outdoors when counts are high. When indoors, keep windows and doors closed and use the air conditioner, if necessary, to stay cool.

Pets

An allergy to a pet can develop at any time, even if the same pet has lived with you for years. Unfortunately, the best antidote is to give the animal away or keep it outdoors. Even then, allergies may still be aggravated for a while. Animal dander and other residue linger in a house for months after the animal is gone. If you must keep a pet, take some precautions. Make some rooms in the house off limits to pets, especially bedrooms. Have the pet sleep in one place, vacuum the bed and around the bed frequently, and wash the bed weekly. Brush the pet outside.

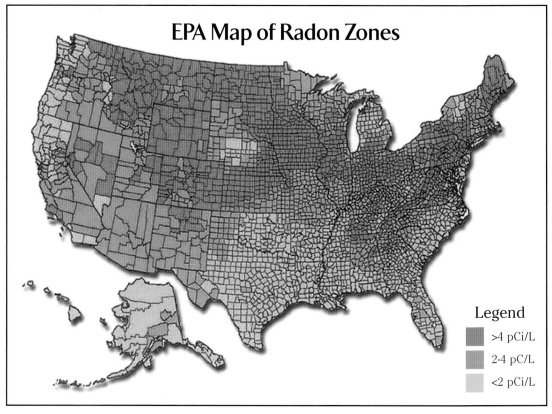

EPA Map of Radon Zones

Legend
- >4 pCi/L
- 2-4 pC/L
- <2 pCi/L

Ideal Radon Levels

Don't be lulled into complacency if radon levels in your house are at or only slightly above the 4 pCi/l recommended level. Even then, there's an increased risk of lung cancer. The healthy home has levels between zero and 1.5 pCi/l, similar to that found outdoors.

Radon

Radon is an odorless, colorless, naturally occurring radioactive gas released from soil and is second only to cigarette smoking as a cause of lung cancer. According to the EPA, as many as 1 in 15 houses has radon levels above the recommended action level of 4 picocuries per liter of air (pCi/l). Closed spaces, particularly, present a problem because radon can build up to dangerously high levels.

Radon is present in all soil to some degree. Basements often act as chimneys (particularly in winter), pulling radon in from areas of high pressure to areas of low pressure. The use of exhaust fans, combustion appliances, and clothes dryers that draw air out of the house, the presence of open fireplaces, inside/outside temperature differences, and wind velocity all influence the degree of depressurization. If a large enough difference exists, the house can literally suck in radon gas through dirt floors, cracks in the foundation, floor drains, sump pits, joints, and tiny cracks or pores in hollow-block basement walls. In locations with permeable or porous soil, houses can pull radon from distances of up to 40 feet.

Radon is a problem in every state of the U.S.A., but levels are higher in some regions than in others. The good news is that a radon problem is not difficult to remedy.

Every home should be tested for radon. Purchase inexpensive test kits at the local hardware store (they cost about $5 each) and place them in the lowest livable level of your house and in all ground-floor bedrooms. If your house has more than one floor, you may wish to take measurements on each floor.

If you find high levels of radon, open windows and stop using rooms containing high levels until you can have the house professionally evaluated. For further help, contact either the National Radon Hotline at 1-800-767-7236, or the National Safety Council's Radon Program at 1-800-644-6999.

When it comes to mitigation, hire a professional contractor experienced in radon reduction. The best radon mitigation specialists will guarantee a reduction in radon levels to below 4 pCi/l. The cost to remedy a severe problem is usually under $1,500. Many states provide a list of qualified, certified contractors. Check with your state's health department or the regional EPA office.

Radon levels can change over time and during different seasons, so a radon test done one year may not be accurate a year later. To be safe, perform tests at different times of the year.

Heavy Metals: Lead & Mercury

The two main heavy metals of concern today are lead and mercury. Small children and unborn babies are the most vulnerable. Brain damage, stunted growth, hearing loss, and blood and kidney disease may result. For adults, even relatively low levels can cause a significant increase in blood pressure. At high levels, lead poisoning can be fatal. Old lead-based paint is the most significant source of lead exposure in the U.S. It's lead dust from chipped paint, not intact paint, that is the problem.

Harmful lead levels can occur when lead-based paint is improperly removed from surfaces by dry scraping, sanding, or open-flame burning. High concentrations of airborne lead particles indoors can also result from lead dust coming from outdoors, including contaminated soil tracked inside, and use of lead in certain activities such as soldering and making

How to Test for Radon

Testing for radon is simple and inexpensive. Most tests involve exposing charcoal canisters to air in the lowest room of your home for 48 to 72 hours and then sending the canister to a lab for analysis.

Unpack the test devices as directed by the manufacturer, and set them on a table or other surface about 3 ft. above the floor. Make sure they are undisturbed and not subject to drafts or fans. Record the test start date and time and location on the included card.

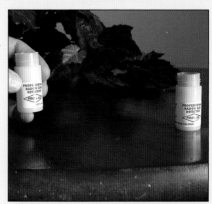

After the test period has passed (usually at least 48 hours), record the end date and time on the card, and pack the canisters in the provided mailing envelope. Send the envelope to the testing lab for evaluation.

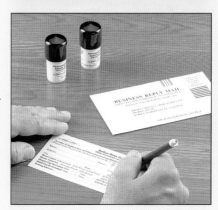

stained glass.

Most homes built before 1960 contain heavily leaded paint. Many houses built as recently as 1980 may contain lead paint. Lead was banned from paint in 1978, but retailers continued to sell old stock until 1980. Unless your home was built after 1980, it is safe to assume it contains some lead paint. Look for it on window frames, walls, exterior siding, and other surfaces.

If in doubt whether paint is lead or not, have a sample tested. You can buy a simple home test kit at hardware stores, or spend a few hundred dollars to have a

How to Test for Lead

When in doubt, it's a good practice to assume that old paint has lead and act accordingly. You can also test for lead with home lead testing kits, but be aware that it is entirely possible to get false negatives from such tests. Follow all directions carefully.

Use a utility knife to clearly expose each layer of paint on the surface to be tested. If you're planning to sand or strip the surface, it's important to test all layers, not just the top.

Rub each layer with a special swab (included in the kit) for 30 seconds. If the swab turns colors (usually pink), lead is present in that layer.

certified lead paint inspector come to your house and test all the surfaces. If lead paint on your house exterior is cracking and flaking, have the soil tested, as well. Contact your state agricultural extension service office for details on soil testing.

If you discover a problem, carefully clean up all paint chips. Clean floors, window frames, window sills, and other surfaces weekly. Use a mop, sponge, or paper towel with warm water and a general all-purpose cleaner. Thoroughly rinse sponges and mop heads after cleaning dirty or dusty areas. Temporarily reduce lead hazards by repairing damaged painted surfaces and planting grass to cover soil containing high lead levels. To permanently remove lead hazards, hire a certified lead-abatement contractor (see page 168). Abatement methods include removing, sealing, or enclosing lead-based paint with special materials. Just painting over the area with regular paint is not enough.

Another heavy metal contaminating the environment is mercury. Elemental mercury is a powerful neurotoxin capable of impairing vision, speech, walking, and writing ability, and causing mood swings, memory loss, and mental disturbances. Just one-seventieth of a teaspoon can contaminate a 25-acre lake to the point where fish are unsafe to eat.

Recent studies show a connection between autism and mercury.

Industrial emissions are a significant source of mercury found in outdoor air and water, but the metal is found around the house, too. Mercury may be found in electrical switches in toys made as late as 2003, fever thermometers, thermostats made before 1980, dental fillings, fluorescent light bulbs, batteries, and many other sources. These products do not pose a health hazard unless the container breaks and the mercury is released. In such a case, mercury vapor is more hazardous than liquid mercury, but both pose a danger.

Carbon Monoxide

Every time something is burned, combustion byproducts are given off. These byproducts are a combination of deadly gases and tiny particulates that are easily inhaled. Wood stoves, fireplaces, candles, kerosene heaters and lamps, cigarettes, and gas ranges are all sources of gaseous contaminants that, if allowed to build up in a house, can cause chronic bronchitis, headaches, dizziness, nausea, fatigue, even death. Of these, carbon monoxide (CO) is the most hazardous. It's the leading cause of death by poisoning in the U.S. today. Carbon monoxide can leak from a broken duct on a furnace, a vent in an attached garage, a malfunctioning gas appliance, or from a blocked or cracked chimney.

The health effects of CO depend on the level and the length of exposure, as well as the victim's health condition. Fetuses, infants, pregnant women, the elderly, and people with anemia or a history of heart or respiratory disease are especially sensitive. Most deaths occur during the winter

months, and most occur while victims are sleeping. Dangerous exposure may occur before you're even aware of the problem. You may get drowsy and doze off, or become so lethargic you're unable to dial 911. High concentrations eventually cause unconsciousness and death. But that's not the whole story. Many people suffer from the flu-like symptoms (headache, fatigue, nausea, dizziness) of low-level exposure without realizing it. If you feel sick at home, but better while away over a weekend or holiday, CO may be the culprit.

If you suspect carbon monoxide is present in your house, open windows and ventilate with fresh air, then leave the premises. If you feel drowsy, call 911 from a neighbor's house. Contact your gas company and public health department to have someone measure carbon monoxide concentrations in all rooms before returning. You, or family members, may require medical attention, so go to the nearest medical emergency center.

Since CO is a symptom of a malfunctioning system or appliance, abatement is straightforward. Have all combustion appliances and the systems that ventilate them inspected by professionals, and fix or replace the appliance or system.

Asbestos

If you live in a house built or remodeled between 1900 and the early 1970s, it's highly probable you're living with asbestos. Once thought to be a miracle substance, this fibrous material was used to insulate walls and heating pipes, soundproof rooms, fireproof walls and fireplaces, strengthen vinyl floors and joint compounds, and give many paints their texture. Asbestos use reached its peak in the 1970s.

Preventing Carbon Monoxide Poisoning

Owners of healthy homes prevent carbon monoxide problems by doing two things.

Have a professional inspection of heating systems prior to the heating season. Include the chimney and flues, and check for proper functioning, leaks, inefficient adjustment, corrosion, blockages, and malfunctioning safety devices.

Buy and use reliable carbon monoxide detectors (cost: between $30 and $50). Position detectors in the hallway just outside every sleeping area where the alarm can be easily heard in the middle of the night.

Asbestos is often found in pipe insulation in older homes. It has a corrugated-cardboard appearance. If the insulation is unbroken, it's safe to leave it in place. If it is damaged, call an asbestos-abatement specialist.

We now know asbestos is no miracle. It's known to cause cancer of the lung, stomach, and chest lining as well as asbestosis, a usually fatal lung disease. Smoking aggravates the disease. Once inhaled, tiny needlelike particles become embedded in tissue where they fester and never leave the body. It may take 15 to 30 years for cancer to develop.

Asbestos poses a health hazard only if fibers are released into the air. Fraying pipe insulation, for example, found in the basements of many older houses releases microscopic fibers. So does cracked or disintegrating fireproof board, often found behind radiators in steam-heated houses and apartments. Even pulling up old vinyl flooring or replacing roofing shingles can release asbestos particles. Once released, asbestos fibers hang suspended in the air, some for more than 20 hours or longer if fans or air conditioners disturb airflow. If not properly removed, these non-biodegradable fibers can pollute the air for the lifetime of the house, becoming airborne whenever dust is stirred up.

If asbestos is undisturbed and undamaged, it is usually left in place (and checked regularly for signs of damage). If asbestos at your house is disturbed or damaged, it should either be removed or contained by certified professionals who can pinpoint asbestos-containing materials and plan a course of mitigation. Never attempt to tear out asbestos-based material yourself; the danger from exposure during removal is much greater than from the low level exposure you face from damaged but undisturbed material. An ordinary dust mask is practically worthless as protection.

The safest plan is to avoid asbestos when you can, and proceed carefully when you can't. If you have any questions about whether something contains asbestos, get them answered by the EPA or local health officials before proceeding (see page 168).

Electromagnetic Radiation

A poorly wired house can lead to all kinds of health problems, including severe headaches, fatigue, and skin disorders. Now that we have so many wires coming into our houses—cable TV, Internet access, telephone, electrical—the potential is high for creating electromagnetic fields that can leave you feeling wired. The illness is called electromagnetic hypersensitivity, and it's already recognized in Sweden where health officials believe over 3 percent of the population suffer from it.

All electrical appliances generate either an electrical or a magnetic field when

Sleep With the Power Off

Sleeping locations should not be back-to-back with refrigerators, televisions, computers, or other appliances that use a lot of electricity. Consider having a "kill switch" installed in all bedrooms to shut down all the electrical circuits to those rooms at night. While this is easy to do in new construction, it isn't too difficult in an existing home, either.

A Healthy Home Has...

- Air unpolluted by smoke, artificial fragrance, or aerosol products.

- Paint and finishers that are low- or no-VOC.

- Carpets that are untreated; installed with a low- or nontoxic backing and either tacked down or glued with nontoxic adhesives.

- Cabinetry, countertops, subflooring, wall structures, and furniture made without urea formaldehyde adhesives.

- 45 percent relative air humidity at temperatures under 70 degrees F.

- House plants to clean indoor air naturally.

plugged in. Even when they aren't in use, an electrical field is being produced. Some appliances generate more elevated fields than others. Refrigerators, computers, televisions, and light dimmers generate intense magnetic fields. Lamps and electric clocks generate magnetic fields, too, though they aren't as high. The good news is the strength of these fields falls off dramatically with distance. Usually just a few feet makes a big difference.

In many homes, improper wiring is to blame. It doesn't matter if the house is old or new. When unequal supply and return currents are unable to cancel each other out, a "net current" is present, and a magnetic field is automatically created. This is a code violation. The best course of action is to hire an electrician to check your home for net current.

You can also use a Trifield gauss meter (about $150; see page 168) to check small-scale magnetic fields in dimmers and three-way switches, as well as in other appliances around the house. If there is a wiring error, this meter is useful in demonstrating the elevated magnetic field. If you find devices with elevated magnetic fields, have an electrician rewire them

correctly. Until you can have the fault repaired, remove them or place them far away from bedrooms or offices.

A magnetic field can come from outside the house, too. High-voltage power lines create huge magnetic fields that can penetrate buildings. This is the most difficult situation to deal with, as there is little you can do to remove the source. However, if you have a power line running across your yard, contact the local utility and ask them to bury it underground. Your initial request will probably go unheeded, but persistence sometimes pays off.

Ventilation

It's definitely worthwhile to identify sources of indoor air pollution and to take steps to reduce the amount of pollution entering your home, but it is just as important that systems for circulating air in your home—the ventilation systems—are functioning properly. A house that breathes correctly can exhale pollution quickly, thus limiting your exposure. See page 112 for more on keeping your ventilation systems in good order.

BUILDING MATERIALS

It seems reasonable to assume that materials used to build our houses are rigorously tested for health effects before being admitted to the marketplace. Unfortunately, that's not the case. Common building materials—like particleboard, insulation, pressure-treated lumber, and adhesives—contain thousands of synthetic compounds suspected of harming human health when released into the air. The healthy solution is threefold: use the most inert, nontoxic material available; provide good ventilation during and after construction; and, if you must live with an unhealthy product, reduce your exposure as much as possible by curing materials before they're installed, and by sealing materials to reduce offgassing.

As with anything else, some building materials are more hazardous than others. This chapter tells you what those materials are and suggests methods for reducing exposure, as well as offering nontoxic alternatives.

How much does it cost to build or renovate with healthy materials? Somewhere between zero and 25 percent more than standard construction, according to experts. Some healthy materials substitutions cost the same as conventional options, such as substituting exterior grade plywood for interior grade. Others cost more initially but are more economical in the long run, such as installing radiant, in-floor heat instead of a forced air system, or using high-quality insulated windows.

Sometimes you'll be faced with difficult choices and no "right" answer. In these instances, it helps to be as informed as possible. Know what your options are and the consequences of each. Understand a commitment to good health requires a change of consciousness. You must reorganize your thinking, know which questions to ask and how to decipher the answers, and perhaps pay a bit more for good health.

What to Watch Out For

When it comes to specifying building materials, health issues are a legitimate concern. Many a person has been pushed over the edge into chemical sensitivity after moving into a new house or renovating a room. No wonder. Today, conventional houses in North America are stuffed with insulation (commonly fiberglass), covered on the outside with medium density fiberboard (MDF) or oriented strand board (OSB), wrapped with building paper, sealed up and sided. The interior may include a layer of drywall taped with toxic joint compounds, then finished with primer and paint. All these materials give off that distinctive "new house smell," actually a riot of synthetic chemicals off-gassing into the air. Here are some of the worst culprits to watch out for.

Asbestos

Asbestos was banned from most U.S. building materials in the late 1970s. But if your house was built between 1900 and 1970, there's a good chance it contains asbestos. If you're remodeling or doing any demolition or removal, you need to be aware of asbestos. Look for it in heating and water pipe insulation, boiler insulation, decorative ceiling tiles, vinyl floor tiles, cement siding and roofing tiles, even in some drywall compounds and particular types of electrical circuitry. This chalky white substance is harmless as long as it remains intact. Danger exists when it

Materials Safety Data Sheets

If you're unsure what is in a building material you wish to use, ask to see a Materials Safety Data Sheet (MSDS). An MSDS is a document prepared by a manufacturer, outlining the procedures for safe handling and disposal of a product. It will also contain information about exposure limitations and specifics on safety equipment. Some manufacturers post them on their Web sites.

While not perfect, an MSDS is a useful tool. In them, manufacturers fulfill their legal requirement to provide a list of chemical substances, precautions for safe handling and use, and known health effects. Because it's not required to reveal all hazards, the MSDS is a flawed instrument. "Trade secrets," for example, are exempt. Inert ingredients (which can account for up to 99 percent of product volume) also need not be listed. Hazardous ingredients present in amounts of less than one percent, and carcinogens present in amounts less than 0.1 percent (the government-established threshold for carcinogens) are not required to be listed.

You can't rely on an MSDS for accurate information on health effects, either. While short-term acute effects may be accurate, information about neurotoxic, reproductive, developmental, cumulative, or synergistic effects is often omitted, as is adverse effects on children.

The best way to use a MSDS is to read between the lines. If no precautions are listed for a chemical and clean up requires only water, chances are the chemical has low toxicity. On the other hand, if gloves, goggles, and a respirator are required for application, you can expect the product to have detrimental health effects once it's fully cured.

Names of chemicals offer further clues. Chlorine, fluorine, and bromine, for example, belong to the halogen family of elements and should be avoided, as should VOCs—anything with "solvent" in the name. Cross-check chemicals for full information. The Internet is a good resource for chemical fact sheets.

Mold & Mildew

Mold is implicated in many sick buildings. It's also been the cause of construction horror stories—uninhabitable buildings, expensive renovations before anyone has even moved in, new buildings razed due to "black mold."

Preventing mold disasters starts as soon as construction begins. Protect all wood and wood products from moisture damage by raising them off of the ground and protecting them with tarps. Cross stack the wood so air circulates around the surfaces. When building or remodeling, never use a material contaminated with mold or mildew. If a material becomes contaminated while in storage or during shipment, reject it.

Be careful with vapor barriers, too. When improperly installed, they can trap moisture on the inside of the building. When combined with drywall (an ideal food), vapor barriers create the perfect environment for mold to run rampant. If your project is rained on, make sure all materials are thoroughly dry before the vapor barrier or tar paper is attached.

becomes water-damaged, dented, corroded, blistered, or otherwise changed in a fashion likely to release fibers into the air.

Be extremely careful with this substance. It's a known carcinogen. The EPA suggests hiring a certified professional to identify and remove all friable or soft asbestos, an expensive project if you've got a lot of it. Some very hard materials may be safe for homeowners to remove, provided you carefully follow EPA guidelines. Never sand asbestos-containing materials.

Encapsulation is another alternative. If you have slightly frayed asbestos pipe insulation, for example, or it has small punctures, wrapping it in several layers of duct tape seals in harmful fibers. When it comes time to sell your house, you'll still need to disclose the existence of asbestos to prospective owners.

Composite Wood Products

Composite wood in residential construction refers to manufactured sheets of material like medium-density fiberboard (MDF), oriented strand board (OSB), and particleboard (PB). These are basically sawdust and wood shavings bonded together by urea formaldehyde glues. Unlike its phenol-based cousin (which is more stable), urea formaldehyde adhesive is concentrated and volatile; it offgasses for months, making it a significant contributor to indoor air pollution. Formaldehyde (a VOC) is quickly becoming known as a severe health hazard in homes and offices. It's one of the main culprits in "new house" smell. Mobile and modular homes, especially, tend to have high concentrations of formaldehyde due to the large amount of composite wood products covering their surfaces.

Some manufacturers are now turning to more benign materials to replace composite wood products. Or, you can simply substitute exterior-grade plywood (which uses phenol formaldehyde) for only a small increase in cost. Ask your builder to air out plywood by cross-stacking it outside before installation, then make sure all sides are sealed with an acceptable vapor barrier sealant (see page 169) to provide the best protection against toxic fumes.

Pressure-Treated Lumber

Pressure-treated lumber (also known as "green board" or "Wolmanized" wood) is often used in residential construction, especially in locations that may be subjected to moisture. Throughout the United States, it's found in decks, fences, building foundations, boat docks, playground equipment, and picnic tables. In the last 30 years, if an exterior wood structure wasn't built of cedar or redwood (both naturally decay-resistant), it was probably built of wood pressure-treated with chromium copper arsenic (CCA), a powerful combination of insecticides and mildewcides that guaranteed that wood wouldn't decay rapidly outdoors. The problem? One 12-foot section of pressure-treated wood contains about an ounce of arsenic, enough poison to kill 250 people.

While Japan, Germany, Australia, and other countries banned or strictly regulated CCA, it became a $4 billion industry in the United States. Fortunately, the EPA halted the manufacture and sale of arsenic-treated wood for most residential uses as of January 1, 2004. Some lumberyards and home centers may continue to sell old stock, however. Always check the tags. Alternatives to CCA are ammoniacal copper quaternary (ACQ) or copper boron azole (CBA) (see page 102).

Vinyl

What we know as "vinyl" is technically polyvinyl chloride, or PVC, a seemingly innocuous plastic receiving lots of attention as one of the most hazardous consumer materials produced. The substance is so bad that virtually all European nations have eliminated some of its uses, and the city of San Francisco and the state of New York have banned PVC pipe for many residential applications.

What differentiates PVC from other vinyls is the addition of a chlorine atom (the C in PVC). Chlorine is the source of many environmental health concerns, such as the creation of dioxin, perhaps the most toxic chemical ever produced. Due to its persistent and bioaccumulative nature (it travels long distances without breaking down and concentrates as it moves up the food chain to humans), dioxin has become a global problem. Many countries have made it a priority to completely eliminate processes that produce dioxin.

Still, over 14 billion pounds of PVC are produced in North America each year, 75 percent of which goes into building materials—piping, siding, roofing membranes, flooring and carpet, ceiling tiles, wall coverings, furniture, electrical insulation, and sheathing, window and door frames, flues, gutters, downspouts, weatherstripping, flashing, and moldings. With the exception of paints and glues, "vinyl" as a product description almost always means made with PVC. When in doubt, ask if it is PVC.

In addition to chlorinated compounds, large amounts of plasticizers (phthalates) are added to make PVC flexible. As much as 60 percent of roofing materials, floor tiles, and wall coverings are phthalates. Because they aren't chemically bonded to the plastic, phthalates leach out into air, water, and other substances with which vinyl comes into contact. Phthalate levels in indoor air in buildings with PVC are typically many times higher than in outdoor air, with concentrations in dust as high as 1,000 parts per million. Like dioxin, phthalates damage reproduction and development in humans and are known carcinogens in laboratory animals.

As if all this weren't bad enough, PVC traps moisture, encouraging mold growth; it releases heavy metals into the air, and is extremely difficult (some say impossible) to recycle. Fortunately, its dangers are being recognized and alternatives are available.

Replacing PVC in a building project is easier than you may think. Some non-chlorinated vinyls (ethylene vinyl acetate or EVA, polyvinyl acetate or PVA, and polyvinyl butyral or PVB) are beginning to be used as substitutes. Many authorities indicate that the absence of chlorine in the formula generally renders these vinyls less harmful than PVC.

Alternatives to PVC are listed on the Healthy Building Network Web site (see page 169). But beware: Some construction materials labeled "green" may actually contain recycled PVC and frequently require virgin PVC to be mixed in with the recycled.

Volatile Organic Compounds

Volatile organic compounds (VOCs) abound in building materials. By their very nature, VOCs offgas into the air. Many of these chemicals are known to cause cancer, damage the nervous system, and suppress the immune system. VOCs are found in plywood, particleboard, wood paneling, carpets and carpet pads, insulation, paints and lacquers, joint compound, finishes, solvents, adhesives, synthetic fabrics, and insecticides. Some of the most common VOCs are toluene, benzene, formaldehyde, and acetone.

When it comes to figuring out which VOCs are offgassing into your indoor air, use the sniff test. Most have some kind of odor. Formaldehyde, for example, has a cloyingly sweet smell, when it has a smell at all. Paint and lacquers emit a familiar "new finish" smell that diminishes with time.

Fortunately, commercial manufacturers now offer low- to zero-VOC, water-based alternatives. When it comes to paint, choose latex over oil, but consider those derived from natural sources, too. Be careful with adhesives and caulk. Though they seem like a bit player in a construction project, they can be the greatest source of short-term VOC emissions.

Product Guidelines

Here are general guidelines for choosing healthy building materials.

Caulk & Adhesives

Caulk and adhesive may seem like a small part of a house, but they can make a big impact on air quality. Solvent-based adhesives have high levels of VOCs, making them harmful to work and live with. Epoxy adhesives are noxious during application but relatively nontoxic when fully cured. White glue (polyvinyl acetate) and carpenter's glue (yellow aliphatic resin) are safe when dry.

Nontoxic alternatives are solvent-free or water-based adhesives. Caulk with a VOC content of 30 grams per liter or less is acceptable.

Cabinets, Doors, Molding, Shelving & Trim

These days, conventional interior cabinets, doors, molding, shelving, and trim is often composite wood covered with veneer to make it look like wood.

How to Seal Prefabricated Cabinets

High-quality and inexpensive prefabricated cabinets are popular choices for kitchen remodeling. There's one problem, though. Most contain composite wood components and are held together with glues that will offgas VOCs long after they're installed. You can have the benefits of these cabinets without the drawbacks, if you're willing to invest some energy in applying a VOC sealer to all surfaces.

Thoroughly coat all surfaces of the new cabinet with a sealer manufactured to prevent VOC offgassing.

Once you've sealed all the surfaces, you can paint the cabinets with no-VOC paint.

Consequently, these products contain large amounts of formaldehyde. In a healthy home, cabinetry, doors, and built-ins are made of solid wood or formaldehyde-free wheat board, (a rapidly renewable resource) and finished with a low-VOC paint or stain. Formaldehyde-free exterior-grade plywood is an acceptable material choice, or use alternative materials, such as metal, for cabinets.

If your cabinets and shelving are made of MDF or other composite wood using urea-formaldehyde binders, seal all exposed sides with a vapor retardant sealer to minimize offgassing.

Subfloors, Sheathing & Underlayment

Subfloors, wall sheathing, countertop underlayments, and some types of wall covering use plywood or other composite wood products. Most composite wood products contain urea-formaldehyde binders that can offgas for years.

When using sheetgoods anywhere in the home, choose low-emission boards such as wheatboard, strawboard, Isoboard, Fiber Tech, Homasote (made from wheat, straw, sugar cane, or recycled paper bonded together with nontoxic agents), or exterior-grade plywood. Seal it with an acceptable vapor barrier sealant and finish with a low-VOC paint. When using plywood in a remodeling project, always choose exterior-grade plywood over interior-grade. The phenol formaldehyde binders of exterior-grade are waterproof and more stable than the urea formaldehyde binders of interior-grade, which are only water resistant. It is best to seal exposed surfaces with a vapor-retardant sealer.

Countertops

Countertops are made up of many components, each of which may contain unhealthy materials. Underlayment, for example, is often composite wood. Covering material (ceramic tile, laminate, etc.) is often glued with toxic adhesives. In a healthy home, countertop finish material is installed over formaldehyde-free underlayment and fastened mechanically, when possible, to avoid the issue of adhesives. All adhesives should be low- or no-VOC and water-based.

When it comes to countertop materials, avoid high-pressure plastic laminates (such as Formica). They contain PVCs and are often attached using high-VOC adhesives. Though more expensive, materials like marble, granite, concrete, ceramic tile, and stone are good choices. Solid-surface synthetics don't offgas, but they are manufactured from petroleum, so they are not necessarily environmentally friendly.

When choosing ceramic tile, it is best to buy glazed or factory-finished tile; on-site sealing may cause exposure to high-VOCs. Be very careful with imported tiles (especially cobalt blue and burnt orange colors); they may contain lead or radioactive materials. Choose large tiles to minimize grout, which is susceptible to mold and staining. Tile should be sealed periodically to resist staining.

Butcher block makes an attractive kitchen countertop, does not require underlayment, and can be mechanically fastened to the cabinets. The porous surface, however, can encourage mold and bacteria growth. Be sure seams aren't

glued with formaldehyde-based adhesives. Finish with an odorless, nontoxic oil such as walnut oil.

Stainless steel and copper are excellent choices but present an issue with creating electromagnetic fields (EMF).

Drywall

Do you know what your walls are made of? Gypsum-based drywall (also known as Sheetrock) is the most commonly used interior wall and ceiling sheathing in modern construction. All gypsum drywall products are natural gypsum sandwiched between two sheets of thin material, generally paper. The 4×8-, 4×10-, or 4×12-foot sheets are attached to the studs, then taped, sealed, textured, and painted. Though economical and convenient, it's not necessarily the best material from a health standpoint. Adhesives and joint compounds offgas irritating fumes (including formaldehyde), and the drywall is subject to moisture damage and mold. Chemically sensitive people often react to the offgassing of inks used in the recycled newsprint comprising the paper facing.

Less toxic solutions include drywall primed with specialty paint or primer to seal off toxic fumes, and joined with joint compound and texture compound made with inert fillers and without formaldehyde and preservatives.

The most natural wall finish (short of adobe) is additive-free plaster. Plaster has the added advantage of blocking VOC offgassing present in the gypsum and taped joints of modern construction. And integrally colored plaster never needs painting. Traditional plaster and lath construction is many times more expensive than drywall—if you can find someone to do it. Fortunately, veneer plaster systems (often called skim plaster) are available that provide many of the same benefits of traditional plaster for a price similar to standard drywall. Veneer plaster is simply a layer or two of plaster installed over special drywall for a smooth, seamless, and impermeable finish.

Flooring

Because it covers such a large surface, nontoxic floor coverings are essential in a healthy home. If you're choosing a floor that would ordinarily be finished on-site, consider a factory-finished product instead. The factory finish allows it to cure outside the home, thus lowering in-home emissions. If you choose to finish it on-site, select a low- or no-VOC, water-based adhesive.

Avoid vinyl flooring. Vinyl chloride fumes emitted from the flooring are a known carcinogen. In a hot or humid environment, the vinyl traps moisture, which can promote delamination of sub-floors and mold growth or rot. In older houses, be careful removing synthetic resilient floors; they may be a source of asbestos.

If you choose a hardwood floor, pay attention to the type of wood. The environmental choice is Forest Stewardship Council-certified wood (FSC). Be sure the underlayment doesn't contain formaldehyde. An installation that requires no glue (as in most traditional hardwood floors), is best, but if the floor must be glued, use water-based glues. Finish the floor with a low- or no-VOC finish.

Look for salvaged, reclaimed, or rapidly renewable products, such as cork or bamboo. Be careful, though. Most bamboo flooring is manufactured in China and may have adhesives and finishes that contain formaldehyde. Do your homework and select formaldehyde-free bamboo. Cork cushions the foot, is durable, sustainable, and provides acoustic and thermal insulation. When using cork, make sure it is not encased in vinyl—see manufacturer's MSDS for information.

All flooring needs to be installed where there is no potential for moisture to seep through a concrete subfloor, like it does in basements and in slab-on-grade homes. This can lead to mold growth and rot. Make sure any flooring installations include a proper vapor barrier and gap between concrete and the flooring material.

Ceramic tile is durable, long lasting, and healthy. Choose large tiles with narrow grout joints, and a grout free of polymer additives. Be sure to seal and maintain it properly. Stone and brick make durable, relatively affordable floors. Don't overlook concrete, especially if one already exists as a subfloor or slab. Painted, pigmented, stained, or acid-etched concrete floors can be works of art.

"True" linoleum (made from wood and cork "flour," limestone dust, pine resin, and colorants mixed with linseed oil from flax seeds and baked onto a jute backing) is a wonderful natural floor covering—durable, resilient, thermally insulating, quiet, and low maintenance, with natural antibacterial properties. Available in sheets or tiles; it doesn't show scratches or cuts and comes with a 30 to 40 year lifespan.

Be wary of all laminated flooring. Some looks like hardwood with veneer or plastic laminated to a composite backing. Others are designed to look like tile or

How to Remove Carpet

There lots of good reasons to remove old carpeting, not the least of which is for your health. If you have allergies or other respiratory ailments, carpet can be your worst enemy. Fortunately, removing carpet is fairly easy (just be sure you wear a respirator). Remove old carpeting and replace it with a natural material that doesn't harbor dust.

You can remove tacked-down carpet with simple hand tools. Begin by cutting the carpet free from the thresholds with a utility knife. Remove the threshold strips with a pry bar.

Use a utility knife to cut the carpet into long strips a couple feet wide. Cut through the pad and the carpet. Roll both up together. Repeat until you've removed all the carpet. This technique disturbs a minimal amount of dust, but be sure to wear a respirator when removing old carpet.

Removing glued down carpet is a little more labor intensive; you'll also definitely need to wear a respirator. Cut the carpet into manageable strips. Use a floor scraper to help remove stubborn adhesive and carpet.

linoleum. Some are bonded with PVCs. Look for laminated floors using biodegradable resins.

Wall-to-Wall Carpet

While wall-to-wall carpet is the most popular soft flooring choice, it isn't the healthiest. A typical carpet contains 120 different chemicals, including formaldehyde, toluene, xylene, and benzene—known human carcinogens. The pad is typically foamed plastic or styrene-butadiene rubber—both petroleum products that offgas for months. For a few days after installation, all new carpets emit air pollutants associated with these chemicals. Though manufacturers claim low-level emissions are safe, not everyone agrees what level is "low." Theoretically, people with asthma or allergies might be more sensitive than the average person. The same people may be affected by dirt, dust mites, and mildew that build up in carpeting. The safest bet is to avoid wall-to-wall carpeting entirely.

Instead of carpet, floors in a healthy home are covered with rugs that can be easily removed and thrown in the washing machine to clean, or given a good shake outdoors and freshened with a bit of sunshine. Choose natural-fiber carpets and rugs, particularly those made of pure wool, cotton, hemp, jute, ramie, sisal, sea grass, or coir with a natural backing, such as felt or jute. The best are certified organic and undyed. Handwoven area rugs—

such as dhurries and kilims—are acceptable if they're untreated and made of natural fibers. Natural fiber modular carpet tiles (which can be installed wall to wall or as a rug) are a decent option, too. If you damage one tile, you can pick it up to clean it or replace it. Just be certain the product hasn't been chemically treated.

Insulation

When properly installed in a well-sealed building envelope, insulation minimizes the energy needed to heat and cool the interior. Resistance to heat transfer is rated according to R-value. If insulation is incorrectly installed, R-value plummets.

When choosing insulation, keep in mind that batts are not as effective as spray-in and loose-fill insulations. Blown-in insulation will not settle the same as loose-fill, making it a better option.

Fiberglass (the most popular type of insulation) is not a healthy choice. It releases both particulates (friable glass fibers) and gaseous contaminants (including formaldehyde). Once encapsulated, fibers are inert; it is during installation or when insulation is exposed or moved that risk of exposure to particulates increases. Use a particle-filter dust mask during handling or installation, and insist that an installer do likewise. Ventilate the house well after installation. Keep the wall cavity dry.

If choosing fiberglass insulation, select one with formaldehyde-free binders or no binders at all. You can choose no-formaldehyde-added fiberglass, or encapsulated batts wrapped in plastic, which makes them heavier and not as friable. However, if you cut the plastic, you will encounter the same fiber issues as with the regular type. If anyone in the house is

Carpet Dos & Don'ts

The healthy home avoids chemically treated carpets, especially those boasting permanent stain resistance, mothproofing, and antimicrobial agents. Stain resistance applied after carpet is manufactured also reduces the quality of indoor air. Nylon and olefin carpets usually don't contain a lot of chemical additives, but they are derived from petroleum, a nonrenewable resource.

If you decide you want wall-to-wall carpet, you'll undoubtedly run across those that are CRI (Carpet and Rug Institute) green labeled, ostensibly providing assurance that the product "is a responsible, low-emitting carpet." Unfortunately, this information isn't as reliable as it sounds because the carpet industry set the standard based on arbitrary maximums for VOCs rather than scientific risk-assessment data. Also, the testing program is voluntary, so you may find a carpet that meets the CRI green standards but isn't labeled.

If you can, air out the carpet for a couple of weeks before installation. Preferably, ask the retailer to unroll the carpet in the warehouse and leave it unrolled for a couple weeks. When it comes time for installation, tack it down instead of using glue. Not only does this facilitate removal, it avoids glue's ill effects. For carpet that needs to be glued down, choose a low-VOC adhesive. After installation, keep windows open and a fan going for two or three days to get rid of pollutants.

Before purchasing any carpet, find out how to treat stains when they occur with nontoxic cleaners. For daily cleaning, a HEPA vacuum cleaner works best; other types re-release into the air as much as 70 percent of what they vacuum up. Or, install a central vacuum cleaner in those rooms with carpet. This greatly reduces the amount of dust stirred up on cleaning day. Deep-clean the carpet annually, at the least, to avoid triggering allergic reactions.

How to Install a Natural-Linoleum Floating Floor

A great alternative to carpet or vinyl flooring is real linoleum, a natural and safe material. Recently, manufacturers have paired linoleum with floating-floor technology to create linoleum tiles and panels that can be installed over any stable subfloor without glue or nails. You can even install it over old vinyl. The panels and tiles snap together using a tongue and groove system. Some types even incorporate a layer of cork for extra cushioning.

Measure your space and order enough tiles or panels plus a few extra boxes. Unpack the tiles and leave them in the room for a few days to acclimate to the temperature and humidity. Prepare the first row by using a circular saw to cut the tongues from the wall side of the first row of tiles. For one corner, cut the tongue off an adjacent side, as well.

The tiles require an expansion gap, so set the provided spacers between the walls and the adjoining tiles. Set the tile you cut two tongues off in one corner against the spacers. Snap the next tile in place (with a spacer) and continue to the end of the row. Cut the last tile to fit, leaving room for a spacer.

For the first tile of the second row, cut a tile to the same size as the last piece of the first row (remove material on the tongue side). Assemble the whole second row. Lift up the front edge and then slide the row against the first row so the second row's tongues mesh with the first row's grooves

When the tongues and grooves are meshed along the whole row, gently push the row down. It will snap into place, making a tight joint. Follow this procedure for subsequent rows, making sure that all joints overlap by at least 8". For the last row, measure and cut tiles to fit, maintaining a gap for the spacers.

chemically sensitive, stay clear of batts backed with asphaltic coatings.

Cotton insulation (some made of shredded blue jeans) comes in batts similar to fiberglass, but is safe to handle and install. It has no formaldehyde-based binders and provides better soundproofing.

Cellulose insulation has potentially higher energy and soundproofing performance and is less harmful to the installer, but with the same R-value as high-density fiberglass batts. Chemicals in the ink of shredded newsprint, however, make cellulose bothersome to some chemically sensitive people.

Today, the most common residential insulation in new construction is spray polyurethane foam (SPF), which has a high R-value, is not ozone depleting, and seals around all penetrations so no vapor barrier is needed. This can offgas if not sealed by drywall or plaster, and some chemically sensitive people may react to it. Rigid foam insulation, popular in the 1980s, offgases badly and should not be used on interior applications. Non-toxic solutions include natural materials, such as cotton, cork (which has a high R-value), and Air Krete, a mineral-based foam.

Framing Lumber

When it comes to framing, choices include standard framing lumber, steel framing, and structural insulated panels. Framing lumber is the most common, and perfectly acceptable from a health standpoint, though not from an environmental one. The house-building industry is responsible for removal of old-growth trees from forests and mountainsides. Advanced framing techniques and optimum-value engineering greatly reduce the amount of wood used in modern construction. Look for the Forest Stewardship Council-certified wood (FSC) logo on wood products which certifies the wood has met rigid environmental standards.

Metal is not a material of choice for framing because it conducts electricity and sets up a large EMR field. Structurally insulated panels (SIPs) is a new technology that allows builders to frame houses with prefabricated insulated wall panels instead of lumber. SIPs might evolve into a healthy option, but current models fall short due to large amounts of adhesives and composite wood used to build the panels.

As an alternative to pressure-treated lumber (CCA), specify recycled plastic lumber (RPL), redwood, or cedar for decks and porches. Check to make sure pressure-treated dimensional lumber, plywood, and engineered beams are treated with less-toxic CCA alternatives, such as Wolmanized Natural Select, Preserve, or Preserve Plus. Borate treated wood has lower toxicity levels than CCA but cannot be exposed to water.

Recycled plastic lumber (RPL) is an environmentally suitable alternative for pressure treated wood if you don't mind plastic covering your deck, porch, or fence. There are several different types—high-density polyethylene, wood-filled, and fiber-reinforced. RPL has a host of advantages: it doesn't require sealing or staining; it holds up well to water, sun, insects, and salty air; it doesn't rot, splinter, or crack; it eliminates the need for paints, stains, or seals; it can be sanded to eliminate scratches, and it has an indefinite lifespan.

Suitable alternatives to pressure-treated lumber are ACQ Preserve (ammoniacal copper quaternary) or CBA (copper boron azole, sold as Wolmanized Natural Select by Wolman). See pages 101 to 103 for more information.

Paints, Sealants & Stains

More than 10,000 synthetic chemicals are used in conventional paints, sealants, and stains. Many are toxic solvents, mildewcides, and fungicides. Such chemical-overburdening is unnecessary. You can now find low- and no-VOC paints, stains, thinners, and waxes made from naturally derived raw materials. There are even low-VOC sealants available for hardwood floors. Choose water-based materials with a low VOC content of 150 grams per liter or less. For those wanting a pure product, old-fashioned milk paint is available in the marketplace. Always vent carefully when painting or sealing and after you are done.

Roofing

The most important attributes in a roof are fire-resistance and durability. Roofing choices vary greatly by region. In the regions where forest fires are common, for example, metal or clay tile roofs make the most sense. In extremely hot and sunny climates, a metal roof is a terrible choice because it absorbs heat. Regardless of region, a metal roof is not recommended near high voltage power lines, due to electromagnetic radiation (EMR) emissions. Look for a roof with at least a forty-year lifespan and low maintenance. In general, choose a lighter-colored roof to absorb less heat and reduce the heat transferred to the home.

Asphalt shingles are safe and durable, offgas outside, and come with a forty-year lifespan. Asphalt in itself is highly toxic

and some chemically sensitive people may react to it even if it's as far away as on the roof.

Flat tar and gravel roofs are not acceptable in a healthy home. They're subject to failure, require frequent replacement, and emit toxic fumes when new.

Clay tiles are acceptable, but consult a structural engineer to make sure roof joists can support the extra weight.

Siding

Exterior wall coverings are as important as interior ones. In a healthy home, natural, no-maintenance materials like brick and stone are preferred. Natural stucco is a good choice; the color is already mixed into the finished coat and it has a long, durable life. Exterior insulation finish system (EIFS, also known as Dryvit) is made by adding a stucco-like finish over foam insulation. It is not a good choice. It can be damaged by impact and traps moisture in the walls if improperly installed, resulting in mold.

Metal siding or corrugated metal panels may be used, but are aesthetically unconventional and not recommended near high power lines due to EMF issues.

Vinyl is not a good choice. It often traps moisture inside the wall cavities, resulting in mold and structural decay. Plus, it's a bad choice from an environmental standpoint, polluting the environment in both its manufacture and disposal.

Hardiboard siding (made of fiber cement), when correctly installed, is fire- and rot-resistant, and it avoids some of the continued maintenance issues of wood.

Then of course there's good old-fashioned wood siding, a good choice from a health standpoint, though it requires maintenance, painting, and is subject to rot.

Windows

Windows are an important feature of a healthy house, providing natural light, views, and ventilation. Choose windows for thermal resistance of the frame, low-maintenance, and durability. Better windows cost more upfront but provide increased comfort, quieter rooms, less fading, and may allow you to downsize your heating/cooling system. Poorly built windows leak, causing loss of energy efficiency. Windows should always be operable to enable ventilation. In general, use double- or triple-pane, preferably insulated glass. Look for U-factors rated by the National Fenestration Rating Council (NFRC). These measure windows' insulation ability. NFRC ratings represent the whole window's performance, not just the glass area.

In addition to U-value, other important factors are the amount of daylight and heat the glazing admits. Glazing that lets in daylight without heat gain is now available, a good choice where solar heating is not the goal.

For health, extruded vinyl windows should be avoided. PVC on the interior will offgas over time. Even though the exterior is maintenance-free, vinyl windows cannot be painted and tend to warp with temperature swings. Because the frames are not strong, more frame is required to hold the glass in place, which reduces the glazing and light area. Better windows are made of aluminum-clad wood, engineered wood, aluminum, and fiberglass.

Most wood windows contain adhesives, and so they need to be finished on the interior with low- or no-VOC sealant to prevent offgassing of formaldehyde and fungicides. Choose prepainted or prestained windows so the factory will capture paint pollutants. Have windows professionally installed, and inspect the flashing and caulking annually.

A Healthy Home Has...

- A foundation tightly sealed against both radon gas penetration and moisture.

- Cast iron, concrete vitrified clay, copper, or high-density piping instead of PVC pipe.

- Solid wood or composite wood sheetgoods sealed on all six sides with a vapor-retardant sealant.

- Walls and ceilings that are covered with materials that are as inert as possible.

- Durable, low-maintenance, healthy floor surfaces such as hardwood, formaldehyde-free bamboo, cork, or true linoleum.

- Cabinetry, doors, and built-ins made of solid wood or formaldehyde-free products.

- Finishes that are low- or no-VOC and nontoxic.

- Insulation that is formaldehyde-free batts, cotton, cork, or Air Krete. Fiberglass insulation, if used, is covered and not bare.

FURNISHINGS & APPLIANCES

It's not easy shopping for safe and healthy furnishings and appliances these days, especially if you're in a hurry or on a tight budget. It's important to do so, though, because the furniture, linens, drapes, major appliances, and office and entertainment equipment in your house can play a major role in your home's health. Be prepared to do your homework, cultivate patience, and shop around.

It also helps to focus on simple and natural items. The healthiest environment has wool, cotton, jute, coir, sisal, or hemp rugs covering the floor. It features solid wood furniture put together without toxic glues and upholstered with organic cotton batting. Untreated cotton is used for draperies, or wood blinds are used instead. Walls are painted to reflect available light. Appliances are well maintained and positioned so that they don't create potentially dangerous electromagnetic fields in living and sleeping areas. All combustion appliances are appropriately ventilated.

Go through your house and evaluate the furnishings you have. Let simple and natural be your guiding principles. As you consider what to replace, begin with furnishings and coverings that you use regularly or that you are exposed to for long periods of time. Obviously, the bedroom is a priority, but if you have a home office or another space where you spend many hours at a time, make it a priority for replacing unhealthy furnishings and coverings.

A good place to begin your healthy home retrofit is the bedroom. At least a third of our lives are spent there. If you live to be ninety, you will have spent thirty years in bed. For sleep to be restful and rejuvenating, this room needs to be truly healthy. Of all rooms in the house, the nursery should be as natural, clean, and safe as possible.

Furnishings

Pay special attention to coverings on walls, floors, and windows. These huge surfaces should not contain chemically unstable materials. Much conventional furniture is made of composite wood products, stuffed with foam, and upholstered with synthetic fabrics chemically treated to resist stains, mold, insects, and fire. While such features may sound desirable, in reality, they are not. Here's what to watch out for when furnishing your home.

Wall & Window Coverings

Wallpaper is not the best choice for a healthy home. Many types are treated with a fungicide, as are the adhesives. Check with the manufacturer before making a selection. If you're concerned about what is in a product, ask to see a Materials Safety Data Sheet (MSDS) or find one online. Avoid vinyl wallpaper, especially. In addition to offgassing a variety of toxins, it stops walls from breathing and can create an ideal environment for mold to grow.

For window treatments, avoid synthetic materials, particularly polyester and fiberglass curtains and vinyl shades. Not only are these chemically unstable, releasing fumes into the air when they get warm, they generate static electricity which attracts dust. If you have these in your home, consider replacing them with natural fiber curtains (organic cotton, linen, silk, hemp), naturally finished wood or bamboo blinds, metallic Venetian blinds,

or homemade rice paper shades. Choose washable materials, not those that need to be dry-cleaned.

Furniture Framing

New wood furniture is often made—at least in part—of some type of composite wood—particleboard (PB), oriented-strand board (OSB), medium-density fiberboard (MDF), chipboard, or plywood. These contain formaldehyde. Don't be fooled by veneers that cover the surfaces. Know what you're getting. Before buying, examine drawer bottoms, dresser and cabinet backs, and other hidden places. When in doubt, call the manufacturer.

Look for furniture made of solid wood. Antiques are a good bet, as composite wood products didn't come onto the scene until after World War II. Furniture more than five years old is a safe compromise, too, as the formaldehyde should have offgassed by then.

The bed is the most important furnishing. Expect to spend quite a bit more for a healthy bed than you would for a conventional one. If you can't afford a healthy bed all at once, start with the pillows, then the sheets, duvet cover, and mattress cover; finally, find a chemical-free mattress and bed frame. The healthiest bed is solid wood with natural finishes and solid wood slats spaced to ventilate the mattress rather than a box

FURNISHINGS & APPLIANCES

spring. The frame shouldn't contain toxic glues, particleboard, or chemical stains or finishes.

Cushioning & Fillers

Most cushions for sofas, chairs, and pillows, and many commercial mattresses are made of or contain polyurethane foam and a variety of undisclosed chemicals used as fire retardants, dyes, pesticides, glues, and fabric treatments, all of which offgas into the air.

Foam mattresses are especially noxious. "Although the label may tell you what the bed is made of, it does not tell you what the materials are made from," explains Walt Bader, president of Lifekind Products in Yuba City, California. For example, polyurethane foam is created by a chemical reaction of polyols and isocyanates (a known carcinogen). With the exception of the steel springs, this kind of bed was created almost completely with synthetic materials derived from petroleum and natural gas.

As foam breaks down with time and normal use, it releases tiny particles into the air, which we breathe in all night long while we sleep. A typical foam and Dacron bed lost half its weight in ten years, going from twenty pounds to approximately ten, according to a study done by the EcoLiving Center, where a natural 20-pound bed lost only two pounds over twenty years. As if all this

Chemical Fire Retardants

Chemical fire retardants are ubiquitous in furnishings today. There are many different kinds with varying degrees of toxicity, but the ones currently drawing the most attention are a group of brominated fire retardants called polybrominated diphenyl ethers (PBDEs). Like PCBs, their long-banned chemical cousins, PBDEs are persistent in the environment and bioaccumulative, building up in people's bodies over a lifetime. They're found in increasing amounts in tap water, household dust, and sewage sludge. In July 2003, researchers found that PBDEs accumulate in breast tissue and are present in breast milk. Although the long-term effects are still unclear, PBDEs are known to be endocrine disruptors that mimic and disturb the actions of hormones.

Though they're found in such everyday products as coffee makers, hair dryers, smoke detectors, and imitation wood products, by far the greatest use of PBDEs is in polyurethane foam for furniture, carpet padding, and mattresses, where PBDEs typically comprise five percent of product weight. Instead of being "bound" into these products, as manufacturers often claim, this chemical has been found in high quantities in dust in residential and business settings.

Toxic flame retardants are banned in Europe. In the U.S., a few major stores have phased them out of their products, including IKEA, Ericsson, Intel, and Philips. In August 2003, the California legislature passed a bill banning these chemicals from consumer products by 2008, but there is no federal law. The EPA is moving to phase out some toxic flame retardants, but that will take a few years. As yet, products containing these chemicals are not required to disclose their content on the label.

weren't bad enough, sleeping on a foam or synthetic fiber mattress retains body heat and acts like an oven, raising body temperature and making sleep lighter. If you're sleeping on a foam mattress, at least encase it in a cotton cover. When it's time to get a new mattress, look for one made of natural materials, such as latex from a rubber tree, certified organic cotton, or pure-grow wool. Ideally, it has no metal springs. Natural materials last longer and keep the body at a more even temperature. A natural latex mattress minimizes movement, a good solution if your bed partner's movement bothers you at night.

If you're allergic to wool, try a pure-grow wool mattress, which naturally repels dust mites. "Those who think they're allergic to wool are actually reacting to the pesticides and chemicals found in commercial wools," says Daryl Stanton, owner of Casa Natura in Santa Fe, New Mexico.

Fabric Finishes

Most conventional fabrics used for upholstery, draperies, and carpets are treated with perfluorochemicals (PFCs) to resist stains, repel water, and provide a nonstick surface. Once thought to be miracles of modern chemistry, PFCs (found in such world-famous brands as Teflon, Stainmaster, Scotchgard, and Gore-Tex) are not so miraculous after all. A flood of disturbing scientific findings since the late 1990s puts them high on the list of chemicals to avoid.

Perflourooctanoic acid (PFOA), a byproduct of decomposing PFCs, never degrades in the environment and once introduced (through water, food, or air)

persists in the body for years. The federal government considers PFOA to be carcinogenic. Low levels are suspected of causing a wide range of tumors on the rise in America today, including those found in the breast, testicles, liver, and prostate. PFOA is known to raise LDL cholesterol levels, thereby increasing the risk of heart attack and stroke.

Many ironing board covers and irons are coated with tetrafluoroethylene plastic, what we know as Teflon. In addition, ironing boards themselves are loaded with flame retardants. When heated, these chemical substances offgas toxic fumes. Look for an iron with a stainless-steel sole plate, which is inherently nonstick. For the ironing board, select a cover and padding that are untreated, undyed, and 100 percent cotton.

Common fabric finishes containing PFOA include carpet and furniture treatments; sprays for leather, shoes, and other clothing; and treatments on ironing board covers and irons. Several environmental groups are lobbying the EPA to remove PFC and PFOA from the marketplace. Until then, it's buyer beware.

Furniture & Mold

This is one occasion when having a healthy home poses a Catch-22-type problem. Furnishings chemically treated to resist mold and mildew are not recommended, yet mold is truly an unwelcome guest. If you live in a hot, humid location where mold is a problem, try to purchase furnishings that aren't upholstered and those that are easily cleaned.

Look for signs of water damage and mold on the backing of all artwork, especially if it is old. If you have furnishings that smell even slightly of mold, have them specially cleaned or replace them. Do so quickly, as mold spreads rapidly and can contaminate indoor air with mold spores that settle in dust and in air ducts.

Fabrics

Most upholstery and drapery fabrics are made of synthetics, such as acrylic or polyester, which are derived from petro-chemicals. In addition, they are loaded with fire retardants, antimicrobial agents, and dyes containing heavy metals. Permanent-press fabrics are treated with formaldehyde, which requires several washings to get it out. All these chemicals continue to offgas for some time. These chemicals can also be absorbed through skin contact.

Polyester is perhaps the worst of these. It's entirely of chemical origin. To give you an idea of its plastic chemical makeup, polyester melts rather than burns. Because polyester doesn't breathe, it can't absorb moisture. Polyester is a principal fiber in pillows, sheets, blankets, and mattresses. Because it can't readily absorb perspiration, people sleeping under polyester blankets report being too cold in winter and too hot in summer. If you wake up in the middle of the night covered in sweat, switch to natural fiber bedding, and the problem will probably go away.

Dress your organic bed with wool-filled pillows and comforters, and sheets made of organic cotton, hemp, or silk. Purchase only bedding that can be washed. Choose pillows made of cotton batting, down, latex, or wool. Natural latex and wool are dust mite resistant. Some people are allergic to down, and some are allergic to latex, so if you're sensitive, ask the manufacturer for a sample so you can test your reaction before you buy.

If you have a PVC shower curtain or shower curtain liner, get rid of it. Install glass panels, or a shower curtain made of hemp, which is naturally mildew resistant and antimicrobial. The next best option is a shower curtain made of organic cotton canvas or 100 percent cotton-duck. Watch out, though, for shower curtains impregnated with antimicrobial or antibacterial treatments containing harmful pesticides.

PVC

Polyvinyl chloride (PVC) is found in shower curtains, mattress pads, flooring, children's furnishings, yoga mats, and car upholstery, to name only a few products. A chlorinated plastic, PVC is a known human carcinogen that generates large amounts of highly toxic waste during production and disposal. It also requires the use of plasticizing agents called phthalates to keep it flexible and soft.

Recent studies link exposure to phthalates to reproductive and developmental disorders, cancer, and organ damage. Phthalates may be at least partially responsible for the high incidence of childhood asthma so prevalent today. Europe recently banned some phthalates. The very best course is to purchase non-plastic furnishings and toys. When you must purchase plastics, look for items made from polyethylene or polypropylene, both of which are nonchlorinated.

Appliances

We continue adding more and more appliances and electronics to our lives, creating a complex and potentially harmful home environment. Because of planned obsolescence, we are constantly burdening landfills with slightly used items that contain heavy metals and other contaminants. Try to purchase solid, long-lasting appliances that can be repaired, not discarded. Keep major appliances in good repair and operate them according to manufacturers' instructions.

Microwave Oven

Whether microwave ovens are safe is still a controversial subject. The latest models appear to be safe, as long as the door closes properly and the seals around the door are clean and undamaged. They do emit high AC magnetic fields, so keep a distance of four to 12 feet away while they're in operation, and keep them a safe distance from food preparation areas. Do not microwave food in plastic containers, even if they claim to be "microwave safe"—plastic leaching into hot fat is the worst combination! Use microwavable glass or ceramic.

Upholstered Furniture

If upholstered furniture is your style, choose custom coverings and furniture stuffed with down and feathers—not formaldehyde-filled foam.

Overstuffed chairs and sofas and soft, yielding mattresses are also bad for posture. Though back problems are endemic in the U.S., we rarely link these problems with our furniture. It isn't necessary to slump in a sofa or hunch over a desk. Sitting cross-legged on the floor is good for you. So is sleeping on a firm surface. Here are a few pointers to consider in evaluating your furniture:

- All furniture should provide a reasonable circulation of air. A 7-inch-thick mattress on a 7-inch-thick box spring does not allow air to circulate. Neither does an overstuffed sofa.
- Seating should be designed to encourage a normal spinal curve to protect against backache. Danish modern designs—wood with simple lines—are good models to follow. Take a look at ergonomic designs.
- Be sure that furniture is strong and free from protruding nails or splintering wood.
- Desks and kitchen counters must be at a reasonable height so you don't have to hunch over while using them.

Cutting Down On Allergens

Avoid wall-to-wall carpet, voluminous drapes, and upholstered furniture in bedrooms, as they vastly increase the level of dust and allergens in the air. Keep the bedroom clean. Wash bedding at least once a week in hot water to get rid of dust mites, and air out bedding for an hour or two in the morning before making up the bed. If you have pets, keep them out of the bedroom and keep the bedroom door closed.

Range

Gourmet cooks insist on gas stoves because they like to be able to control the heat of the burner. Clinical ecologists, on the other hand, contend that gas ranges are a major source of pollution in the home. If you prefer gas and no one in your house is sensitive to the fumes, be sure you have a ventilated range hood, vented directly to the outside (hoods that "filter" and recirculate are useless), and adequate cross ventilation in the kitchen.

Electric stoves are safer for sensitive people and are cleaner to operate. Higher end models offer nearly as much control over heat as gas models. When shopping for an electric range, choose a simple one, as many extra features aren't so healthy. Self-cleaning and continuous-cleaning types, for instance, release noxious fumes. The best way to clean an oven is to wipe it down after every use and clean it with a homemade cleaner (see pages 69 to 81).

Dishwasher

Do not use soaps containing chlorine or fragrance, or substances touted to remove water marks on glassware. They only add chemicals to the dishwater that can be released into the air when the dishwasher is opened. Use a nontoxic, fragrance-free, biodegradable dishwashing soap. When shopping for a dishwasher, look for models that run quietly.

Refrigerator

New refrigerators may run quietly, but they don't run cheap. The next time you buy a new refrigerator, look for one that's energy efficient. Since refrigerators use so much electricity, they generate a great deal of EMR. To limit exposure, place the refrigerator on an outside wall. If that is not possible, be sure the room on the other side of the wall is infrequently used to prevent exposure to large amounts of EMR. The worst place for a refrigerator is on a wall that adjoins a bedroom or home office.

Keep the cooling coils clean or they become coated with dust. If your refrigerator is self-defrosting, be sure to empty the drip pan (located underneath the unit) often and clean it out monthly; otherwise, it is an ideal culture for mold.

Electronics

The main component of most family rooms is a television big enough for the entire family to view. Because television sets emit radiation (from the screen, sides, and back), sit at least three feet away from the set; some experts recommend children sit nine feet away. As a

Electromagnetic Radiation (EMR)

Until more facts are in concerning the dangers of EMR, it's best to minimize the number of electronic gadgets in your house, especially if you or any member of your family is "electrically sensitive." As a general rule, don't have anything plugged into an electrical socket in the wall immediately at the head of the bed. Move digital clocks and halogen lamps at least six feet away from the bed. And make sure you don't have a refrigerator, computer, or television set on the other side of the adjoining wall. Next time you're choosing a new bed, choose one without metal springs, which conduct electricity.

general rule, the larger the screen the stronger the fields. If possible, choose a flat-screen LCD or plasma television over a traditional set. These models generate fewer potentially harmful electromagnetic fields.

Like television sets, computers can emit strong EMRs. Cathode ray tube (CRT) computer monitors, especially old ones, emit small amounts of radiation. Place seating at least 30 inches away from the front of the screen and 40 inches away from the sides and back. Liquid crystal display (LCD) screens have lower EMRs and don't flicker and cause eyestrain in the way CRT monitors can. LCDs have dropped dramatically in price, and are a very good upgrade.

Load up your desk with other electronics—fax, scanner, printer—and you're increasing your exposure to EMR, as well. The best layout is to put as much office equipment as possible on the opposite side of the room from your desk, and make sure all electronics are properly shielded and grounded. Unplug those you don't use often.

Cordless phones and cell phones may pose a risk, too. While traditional corded telephones are wired directly into the telephone system (and generate small AC magnetic fields), cordless and wireless phones use radio and microwave frequencies to transmit. Because these phones are held close to the head, the user is exposed to low-intensity radiation that may have a deleterious effect on the brain. Until more research is done, it's smart to use traditional phones whenever possible, limiting the use of cordless and cell phones to travel and emergencies, and then using an earpiece to increase

the distance between the phone and your head. If you use a cell phone as your primary phone, consider purchasing a cell phone dock that will enable your cell phone to ring through a traditional phone (see page 169). This will allow you to talk on your cell phone without holding it anywhere near your head.

Washers and Dryers

Like refrigerators, washers and electric dryers generate high AC magnetic fields when in use, so keep them away from sleeping areas, home offices, and other rooms where people spend a great deal of time.

The best washers are front-loading; they require less water and less detergent, and they tend to be gentler to clothes. Avoid those with plastic interiors, if possible. Stainless steel and porcelain-on-steel interiors are preferred.

Caution: Cell Phones

There is some concern of harmful health effects from long-term cell phone use. Because of the short distance between the phone and the user's head, cell phone users are exposed to low levels of radio frequency energy (RF), which may cause brain tumors and other ill effects. "There is no proof that wireless phones are absolutely safe," according to a Samsung cell phone user guide.

Wireless phones emit low levels of RF in the microwave range while being used, as well as very low levels of RF in standby mode. Most biological research has focused on high levels of RF (which are harmful), so more studies need to be done before absolute safety can be determined. In the meantime, to be safe, it's best to use an earphone attachment when using your cell phone because exposure to RF is drastically lower when distance from the source is increased.

Hidden Bathroom Hazards

Avoid colored towels and toilet paper. These are usually dyed with chemical dyes containing benzene, coal tar, and formaldehyde. Even white towels and toilet paper are bleached with chlorine to make them bright white. The best choice is certified organic cotton towels and bath mats. Next best is 100 percent cotton, which may nevertheless contain pesticide residues. Toilet paper should be bleached without chlorine, unscented, and not dyed.

If your kids play with bathtub toys, check toys periodically for mold.

Check under the washer periodically for leaks and any visible sign of mold growth. Broken hoses on washing machines are a common cause of major water damage. If hoses are dry or appear cracked, replace them with high-quality braided metal hoses. If you discover a damp floor, clean it well. If you think mold has taken hold in the flooring, have a mold abatement specialist do a thorough evaluation and recommend a course of action.

Discourage mold from forming inside the washing machine by leaving the machine door open for a few minutes after each use so it can dry out thoroughly.

When it comes to dryers, electric units are the healthier choice. Whether gas or electric, all dryers must be vented directly outside. Make sure that the vent is not located near an open window or other vent into the house, or lint, moisture, and odors will end up right back in your house, possibly causing allergic or asthmatic reactions. Be sure to clean the dryer filter after each use to prevent fires and reduce the amount of particles in the air. The most natural (and least expensive) way to dry clothes is, of course, outside on a clothesline where they receive both fresh air and sunshine.

A Healthy Home Has...

- Furniture and coverings that are simple and natural.

- No PVC of any kind.

- A minimal amount of human-made electro-magnetic radiation (EMR).

- No dangerous synthetic fabrics.

- Beds made of solid wood with natural mattresses and bedding (no metal springs).

- Furniture padded with untreated cotton batting instead of foam.

- Untreated draperies of natural fibers or wood blinds.

- Solid wood furniture with natural finishes.

- Above all else, healthy bedrooms.

HOUSEKEEPING

There is one major source of indoor pollution found in nearly every house and apartment in America: That giant cache of household cleaners used to take care of the daily needs of house and yard. The chemicals in these products pollute indoor air with vapors and fumes that hang around for days, especially if the house is poorly ventilated. They also eventually pollute our waterways and find their way into drinking and bathing water coming out of the household tap.

Whether they enter the human body through the air or through water, they create imbalance. Chemicals contained in some of these products have been found to be neurotoxic, meaning they disrupt brain and nerve functions. Others are suspected of causing cancer, reproductive problems, and birth defects. Still others cause respiratory ailments and eye, nose, and skin irritation. A vast majority of them, when inhaled, have a wide range of psychological effects, making us feel sluggish, dizzy, nauseated, confused, or depressed.

Though small doses of these substances probably won't harm you, no one knows about the combined, long-range effect. We may ultimately find that many "inexplicable" neurological diseases are the result of long-term low-level exposure to toxic chemicals.

Cleaners

Though you can't create a 100 percent nontoxic environment in today's world, you can take steps toward minimizing the poisons you do have in your home. The best place to start is with cleaning products—oven cleaners, furniture polish, disinfectants, degreasers, all-purpose cleaners, and so on. Box up any commercial products you currently have and store them in the garage until you can dispose of them properly. Replace those smelly, synthetic chemicals with more natural products that can clean and disinfect with spectacular results and without harmful side effects.

When you need to purchase a cleaner, think about health, not cost, before you buy. Buy the least hazardous product, not the least expensive product. If you must purchase a poisonous chemical, do so responsibly. Buy only as much as you need to do the job at hand. Make sure there is plenty of ventilation while using it—open windows and turn on exhaust fans. Store it so it won't evaporate and pollute the air inside your house. Remember, the poison you bring into the house is your responsibility as long as it rests underneath your roof. Take care to dispose of it properly.

Learn how to read labels. Federal law requires manufacturers of hazardous products to post caveats—signal words— on their labels, along with the name of the hazardous substance and a description of the hazard (such as "causes burns" or "absorbed through the skin"). The words "DANGER" or "POISON" indicate a highly toxic, corrosive, or extremely flammable product. The words "WARNING" or "CAUTION" indicate a moderate or slight toxicity, appropriate for products unlikely to cause permanent damage when first aid is given.

Be wary of the word "nontoxic." It's an advertising word and doesn't mean the product is entirely free of hazardous ingredients. Read the whole label for health warnings, and use good judgment. In general, look for products that are biodegradable and contain natural ingredients—they're likely to be healthy.

Drycleaning

An often-overlooked source of indoor air pollution is dry-cleaned clothes. Harsh solvents such as carbon tetrachloride, perchloroethylene, trichloroethane, naphtha, benzene, and toluene can fill a house with vapors for a week or more after clothes are brought back from the cleaner. If you have items dry-cleaned, remove the plastic bag as soon as possible and air the items outdoors for at least six hours before bringing them inside.

An alternative to standard dry cleaning is a process called "wet cleaning" which depends on computer-controlled washers and nontoxic detergents. Another healthy process uses liquid carbon dioxide.

Avoid dry cleaning altogether by using natural fabrics (like cotton, wool, silk, hemp) laundered with natural soaps. Such care extends the life of the fabric and keeps colors truer than dry cleaning does.

Other Household Products

Aerosol Sprays

This is a straightforward choice. Avoid aerosol sprays, including hair spray and spray paint. They can disperse the product in tiny droplets that can be deeply inhaled into the lungs and quickly absorbed into the bloodstream. In addition, aerosols ignite easily, and cans may explode when subjected to high temperatures or pressure.

Bleached Paper

Common varieties of paper towels, toilet paper, coffee filters, tampons, and dozens of other paper products fall into the bleached-paper category. To get paper whiter than white, manufacturers use copious amounts of chlorine. Bleached paper may also contain dioxin, one of the most toxic materials known, capable of causing toxic effects at exposure levels hundreds of thousands of times lower than most other chemicals. The solution is simple: Use unbleached or oxygen-bleached paper.

Plastic Food Containers

Keep plastic away from food whenever possible. Most plastic products contain plasticizers to enhance flexibility. Animal studies suggest these chemicals may harm the reproductive system. When you store or wrap food in plastic, trace levels of plasticizers migrate into the food. High acid content, high fat content, and heat accelerate the process. Cooking oils, in particular, pose a concern. Reduce your exposure by purchasing cooking oil in glass bottles. The same holds true for microwaving food in plastic containers. Use only containers and wraps labeled microwave-safe, or use glass containers and cover foods with parchment or waxed paper.

Since a healthy home avoids all known carcinogens, it's particularly wise to stay away from anything that brings PVC into contact with food. Vinyl chloride has been found to leach into foods and beverages stored in flexible plastic containers and wraps. Cooking oils, in particular, when stored in PVC bottles appear to be highly toxic when heated. In addition, PVC bottles are not recyclable—still more

---

Chemical Carpet Cleaning Machines

Cleaning carpets with cleaning machines that use harsh detergents and solvents invariably fill your house with chemicals—a high price to pay for cleaner carpet. Steam- or hot-water-only cleaners cut through dirt without chemicals. While commercial models generate steam hot enough to kill germs, you can't count on the average household model (costing from $50 to $100) to do an adequate job of sterilizing. But that's okay. As soon as you walk over a surface again you've got more bacteria, anyway. Make sure all treated areas are dry within thirty minutes, so they won't become a breeding ground for more bacteria, fungi, or dust mites.

---

reason to avoid them. Look on the bottom of the bottle. If the recycling code is the number three (often found next to the three-arrow recycling symbol), the bottle is made of PVC.

Plastic Baggies & Bottles

Baggies and bottles can be used and reused as long as they are thoroughly cleaned and dried so bacteria does not grow. The best plastic bottles are polycarbonate or Lexan, a durable, glass-like, non-porous plastic that doesn't leach into what's contained inside.

Hazardous Product Storage & Disposal

The average American home has some 100 pounds of hazardous household products stowed in its basement, garage, storage shed, and closets. Chances are your house is no exception. As you begin to clean and unclutter your surroundings, you'll undoubtedly have questions about how to store those few hazardous products you feel you need to keep, as well as

Types of Hazard

Hazardous household products are separated into four categories according to type of hazard.

Type of Hazard	Definition	Common Products
Corrosive	Products that eat away or dissolve other materials, damaging the body or environment.	Bleach, drain cleaner, lye, oven cleaner, solvents, batteries.
Explosive/Reactive	Can detonate or explode through exposure to heat, sudden shock, pressure, or incompatible substances.	Drain cleaner, ammonia (when mixed with bleach), bleach (when mixed with acids or alkalies), chemical fertilizers, some pool and spa chemicals, aerosol sprays, petroleum-based solvents and degreasers. Old ionizing smoke detectors contain radioactive material.
Flammable	Products that catch on fire easily and burn intensely.	Cans of spray paint, house paint, motor oil, gasoline, kerosene, nail polish, hairspray, furniture cleaners, butane gas.
Toxic	Capable of causing injury or death through ingestion, inhalation, or skin absorption. Some toxic substances cause cancer, genetic mutations, and fetal harm.	Bleach, hair dye, some air fresheners, moth repellants, rubbing alcohol, nail polish, paint fuels, antifreeze, lead or nickel-cadmium batteries, thermostats and thermometers containing mercury, some fluorescent lightbulbs, among many other household products.

how to dispose of others so harmful you don't want them under your roof any longer.

The first line of defense against hazardous waste is to avoid using harmful chemicals in the first place. If you must keep some hazardous chemicals under your roof, store them in as few places as possible, keeping items of like kind, purpose, and safety level together. Do not store pesticides in the pantry, for example, or dog food next to charcoal briquettes. Try to keep very hazardous substances together, apart from relatively safer ones.

If there are children or pets in the home, store dangerous products on high shelves, in locked cabinets, or in cabinets with childproof latches. Storage places should be cool, dry, and not subject to freezing.

The bathroom medicine cabinet makes a great first project. Keep medicines in their original containers and store them on the top shelf, where children can't see them. If any container or bottle lacks a label, throw it away. Put a lock or childproof latch on the door.

Americans generate 1.6 million tons of hazardous household waste per year. What becomes of it? The typical household does one of five things—dumps it down the drain, pours it on the ground, dumps it down storm sewers, throws it out with the trash, or stores it in the basement indefinitely because no one knows what to do with it. All these methods pose

Hazardous Waste Disposal

This chart should be used only as a guide. Contact your local officials to determine what disposal options exist in your area.

Automotive Products	Flush	Trash	Recycle	Reuse	Save for Collection
Antifreeze			*		
Gasoline					*
Kerosene			*		*
Motor oil			*		*
Windshield wiper fluid					*
Pesticides					
Fertilizer					*
Flea collar and spray					*
Fungus control chemicals					*
Insect-control chemicals					*
Home Improvement Products					
Adhesive and glue (solvent-based)					*
Adhesive and glue (water-based)		*			
Paint brush cleaner (solvent-based)				*	*
Paint (water-based latex)				*	*
Paint (solvent-based oil)				*	*
Paint thinner				*	*
Paint remover/stripper					*
Putty/grout/caulk		*			
Stain and varnish				*	*
Cleaners					
Ammonia-based	*				
Bleach-based	*				
Disinfectant	*				
Drain Cleaner	*				
Floor stripper					*
Furniture polish					*
Glass cleaner	*				
Metal cleaner					*
Oven cleaner					*
Spot cleaner					*
Toilet bowl cleaner	*				
Window cleaner	*				

Air Out, Air Dry

Never underestimate the goodness of hanging clothes, linens, pillows, rugs, mattresses, and upholstered cushions outside to air. The twin gifts of sunshine and fresh air help keep these items in top-notch condition, discouraging mildew and pests. Ultraviolet rays are germicidal, too. It's best to air out items before storing them for the season; then air them out again before using them. Such a routine is a return to simplicity, walking the soft path instead of relying on technology. While you're at it, let sunshine into your home by taking down heavy draperies blocking winter light and opening windows to sun and air.

When you wash carpets or fabrics that you wish to preserve from fading, dry them out of direct sunlight. If you wish to sun bedding, carpets, and upholstery for hygienic reasons, you will have less fading if you do so while they are dry.

a threat to the quality of our water, our air, and our soil—which eventually comes around to threatening people and animals on the planet. Even empty containers of hazardous materials can pose hazards to sanitation workers, septic tanks, or wastewater treatment plants because of residual chemicals that might remain.

If a chemical product must be used, find out the best method for disposing of it so it causes as little harm as possible. In most cases, the best thing to do with a leftover product is to use it up, share it with a friend, or find a business or organization that can use it.

If a product can be poured down the drain, be sure to flush with plenty of water. Be extremely careful if you have a septic system, as this waste will not pass through a treatment plant, but will go straight to your drainage field.

Products suitable for landfill disposal can go in the trash. Empty containers can be thrown away, but liquids should never be disposed of in the trash. Some products (like paint) are acceptable for landfill disposal if they are hardened or dried up. Contact your local official before throwing away any product of concern.

For many hazardous products, no safe disposal method is available. These must be taken to a special collection facility or stored safely until your community holds a household hazardous waste collection day. Each community is different, so call your local environmental, health, or solid waste agency about programs and services in your area.

Corrosives

Keep corrosive products—such as drain cleaner, oven cleaner, and lye—together. If a container begins to corrode, place the entire container in a plastic bucket or glass jar with a tight-fitting lid. Pack non-flammable absorbent materials, such as clay-based kitty litter or vermiculite, around the container. Clearly label the outside container with contents and appropriate warnings, then dispose of it at local hazardous-waste disposal center.

Flammables

Exercise caution with extremely flammable products, such as gasoline and kerosene. These should be stored in approved containers in an approved storage locker. At the very least, they should be stored outside the house, in a well-ventilated unattached garage or storage shed, away from all sources of heat, flame, or sparks, or sources of ignition, such as pilot lights, switches, and motors. The best disposal method for these products is to use them up. Share them with friends or neighbors if you can't use them all yourself. You can take used motor oil to a hazardous waste center or auto parts or oil change stores.

Toxic Cleaners

Most liquid commercial cleaners release harmful vapors into the air. Store these with tight-fitting caps and lids in a well-ventilated area away from the kitchen and living and sleeping areas. Always follow instructions on the product label for safe use and disposal. Keep the phone number for your local poison control center by the telephone, and have the label handy to read over the phone should an accidental poisoning occur.

When disposing of toxic cleaners and polishes, wrap the empty containers in newspaper and throw them out with the trash. Some communities allow this disposal method for indoor pesticides and fertilizers as well.

Paint

Store cans of paint in one place, upside down, with tight-fitting lids (storing them upside down means the pigment will settle at the top of the can so it will be ready to use when you open it). Keep from freezing temperatures. The best disposal method is to use up paint or give it away to someone who can use it, such as a theater group or community center. If you live in larger community, your local waste removal service may have a site where you can drop off unused paint. If there is a small amount of latex paint left in the can, open the lid and let it air—in a well-ventilated area away from children and pets—until the paint dries hard. Then wrap the can in newspapers and put it out with the trash. Oil-based paint must be taken to a hazardous waste collection center.

Electronics & Appliances

Circuit boards and cathode ray tubes (CRTs) contain heavy metals and other toxic materials. These items need to be recycled, not dumped, to reclaim and contain these hazards. In some communities, nonworking computers are picked up with curbside recycling. Several companies will safely dispose of or recycle your computer. Many will accept obsolete equipment for a small amount per pound. Check with your local waste disposal company. Some computer manufacturers—including Dell,

Storing Fabrics

Instead of toxic mothballs, try herbal remedies. They are effective and leave woolens smelling good. Natural repellents include dried lavender, cedar chips, tobacco leaves, pennyroyal leaves and stems, and pyrethrum daisy flowers.

Herbal remedies work only if the clothes are clean and stored in airtight containers that stay closed for several days at a time. At least once a year, take everything out of the drawers and closets for a good airing. Unfold individual items, and give each a good shake. Then hang them out in the sun and breeze for a few hours. Store with a fresh herbal sachet. It helps to give sachets a little squeeze from time to time, to release a fresh burst of scent.

Common Hazardous Household Products

Automotive—Gasoline, motor oil, antifreeze, windshield wiper fluid, car wax and cleaners, lead-acid batteries, brake fluid, transmission fluid, and power steering fluid.

Home improvement—Paint, varnish, stain, paint thinner, stripper and stripped residue, caulk, and adhesives.

Yard—Insecticide and insect repellent, weed killer, rat and mouse poison, pet spray and dip, flea collars, and wood preservative.

Cleaners—Furniture polish and wax, drain opener, oven cleaner, tub and tile cleaner, toilet bowl cleaner, spot remover, bleach, ammonia, mothballs, and disinfectant.

Other—Household batteries, cosmetics, pool chemicals, shoe polish, lighter fluid, prescription medicines, arts and crafts materials.

HP, and IBM—can recycle your machine, though some do so only when you buy a new one. Consider donating working equipment to charity; check your phone book for local organizations. Of course, you'll want to be sure the hard drive is wiped clean first, to protect your privacy.

Toner and ink cartridges can be also be recycled; Staples and FedEx-Kinko's shops nationwide accept toner and ink, as do other businesses. Some charities collect used cartridges as part of their fundraising.

Batteries contain a variety of toxic chemicals and heavy metals and should be recycled rather than thrown in the trash. Pharmacies and drug stores typically take button batteries, like those used in watches and hearing aids. Office supply stores sometimes take nickel cadmium (NiCad) rechargeable batteries.

Check with your sanitation department for disposal of large items, such as washers, dryers, and ranges. There may be local rules on disposing of appliances that use CFCs, like air conditioners and refrigerators. If your area doesn't collect large items, call your local solid waste agency to schedule a pickup, which often comes with a charge. Some retailers will recycle old appliances when you purchase a new one, but may charge a fee. Landfills or scrap metal dealers may take appliances for a fee.

Make Your Own Cleaning Solutions

While you can buy organic and natural cleaners, it's cheaper and more fulfilling to make your own. Simple ingredients often do the trick just as effectively as laboratory concoctions. Most recipes are no-mess, no-fuss, and are made with simple ingredients you probably already have in your cupboard.

Ingredients

The big five ingredients you'll need are a natural scouring cleaner like borax or Bon Ami, distilled white vinegar, baking soda, salt, and lemons. All these are non-chlorinated, ecologically safe substances that are available in supermarkets.

If you want more options for recipes, add some cornstarch and washing soda (available at the grocery store) to your list of ingredients. On the few occasions you need a heavy-duty cleaner, use TSP (trisodium phosphate), available at hardware stores. TSP, a minor skin irritant, is moderately toxic if ingested. It does not produce toxic fumes, but it does pollute waterways with phosphates. Use TSP sparingly and always wear rubber gloves. Don't stop reading labels when you shop for these things, though. Some brands of cleaner identified as TSP are actually sodium metasilicate. They may not work as well as TSP, and present their own health hazards.

Most of the cleaners described below work best when freshly mixed. If you choose to store them, tighten the lids and put them in a cabinet equipped with a childproof latch.

Tools

The tools you'll need to make your own cleansers are as simple as the ingredients. You'll want to have the following on hand:

- Glass or stainless steel bowls
- Glass or stainless steel measuring cups
- Stainless steel measuring spoons
- Pumice stone
- Spray bottles, glass or plastic
- Sugar shaker, glass or plastic
- Glass jars with tight-fitting lids
- Plastic or metal funnel
- Silicone-treated dust cloths
- Bottle labels

The Basics

All-Purpose Castile Cleaner

½ tsp. washing soda (optional)
2 tsp. borax
½ tsp. Castile soap

It only takes a handful of natural ingredients to replace an arsenal of toxic cleansers. For basic cleaners, keep borax, distilled white vinegar, baking soda, salt, and lemons on hand. Essential oils of eucalyptus, lavender, citrus, pine, tea tree, and white cedar are also useful for some recipes.

Keep these basic tools on hand for mixing and applying natural cleaners.

Tools

Cleaning tools like mops and sponges should also be selected with an eye toward health and safety. Select durable natural, cleaning tools, such as:

- Cotton and hemp cloths rather than paper towels or disposable wipes
- Containers made of glass and/or plastic
- Cotton mops with wooden handles
- Natural sponges
- Brooms with wood handles and natural bristles

2 cups hot water

10 drops essential oil

Mix all ingredients in a spray bottle and add enough hot water to fill. Spray surfaces as needed and wipe clean with a natural sponge or cotton cloth. Cleans almost every surface in the home.

Dishwasher Soap

1 part borax

1 part washing soda

Mix the two and use the mixture in your dishwasher in place of commercial detergent. If you live in a hard-water area, you may have to adjust the proportions to avoid formation of soap film on the dishes. Or grate pure bar soap, such as Ivory, into a quart of water, and liquefy in a blender. Store in a tight glass container. Add white vinegar to the rinse water to give glasses an extra shine.

Drain Opener

To avoid clogging drains, use a strainer to trap food particles and hair, collect grease in cans rather than pouring it down the drain, and pour a kettle of boiling water down the drain weekly to melt fat that may be building up in the trap.

To open a clogged drain, put ½ cup baking soda and then ½ cup white vinegar down the drain. Cover the drain and let sit for a few minutes, then pour a kettle of boiling water down the drain to flush it.

All-Purpose Cleaner

½ cup borax

1 gallon hot water

Mix ingredients in a bucket until borax is thoroughly dissolved. Use in areas that need general cleaning and wipe clean with a sponge or rag. Store in a spray bottle for everyday use.

General Disinfectant

2 quarts apple cider vinegar

Small handfuls of dried lavender, rosemary, sage, rue, or mint

Mix all ingredients in a 2 quart jar and cover tightly. Let sit for at least four weeks and strain out the herbs. Pour into a spray bottle. Spray anywhere that's ripe for germs—such as places where lots of hands have touched, or in a sick room.

Sanitizer

A solution of 70 percent isopropyl alcohol and 30 percent water is a great disinfectant, much better than 100 percent alcohol. However, alcohol is highly flammable, so use with caution.

Mildew Remover

½ cup vinegar

½ cup borax

1 gallon warm water

Dissolve vinegar and borax in water. Clean mold and mildew with wet sponge and towels. Mix fresh for each use.

Surface cleaners

Hardwood floors

To clean and shine, mix ¼ cup white distilled vinegar with one gallon warm water.

Linoleum floors

Mop with one cup white vinegar mixed with two gallons water to remove greasy film. Polish with club soda.

Oven

For spills in the oven, let the oven cool for a couple minutes, then sprinkle salt on the spill right away. Let it cool for a few more minutes, then scrape the spill away and wash the area clean. Or wipe oven down while still warm with a soapy cloth.

Cleaner Ingredients for Cleansers

These items are all you need to make any of the recipes in this chapter.

- Baking soda: Absorbs odors, deodorizes, is mildly abrasive.
- Beeswax: Turns formulas into pastes for shining and waxing.
- Bicarbonate of soda: Shines stainless steel and hardwood floors.
- Bon Ami: Abrasive cleaning powder containing calcite and ground feldspar.
- Borax: Naturally occurring alkaline mineral that loosens dirt and stains and removes odors.
- Castile soap: An unscented vegetable-based soap that comes in liquid or bar form.
- Club soda: Removes stains.
- Cornstarch: Absorbs moisture.
- Distilled white vinegar: Neutralizes stains and odors. Choose grain-based (not petroleum) unless the recipe calls for cider vinegar.
- Isopropyl rubbing alcohol: Disinfectant.
- Lemon juice: Whitener and deodorizer.
- Olive, mineral, and canuba oil: Wood cleaners.
- Salt: Absorbs oil and dehydrates bacteria when combined with water.
- Toothpaste: Polishes and buffs metal, especially silver.
- Washing soda: Removes grease and dirt.

Scouring Powder

Sprinkle borax, baking powder, or dry table salt on a damp sponge. Scour and rinse.

Tiles & Porcelain

Clean tiles, toilets, baths, and sinks with bicarbonate of soda and a damp cloth.

Toilet Bowl Cleaner & Deodorizer

Baking soda
Vinegar

Sprinkle some baking soda into the bowl. Drizzle with vinegar; scour with a toilet brush.

Polishes

Aluminum

To remove stains and discoloration from aluminum cookware, fill cookware with hot water and add two tablespoons cream of tartar to each quart of water. Bring solution to a boil and simmer ten minutes. Wash as usual and dry.

Brass

Clean and polish unlacquered brass to a shine with a soft cloth dampened in Worcestershire sauce.

Copper

Combine vinegar and salt. Apply the mixture to copper surfaces with a rag and rub clean.

Chrome

Hard lime deposits around faucets can

Caveat

Ammonia can damage the lungs when inhaled, and when mixed with bleach forms a toxic gas; it should be avoided. Most of the general cleaners listed in this book—drain, all-purpose, furniture, and metal—replace any product you may buy that contains ammonia.

be softened for easy removal by covering the deposits with vinegar-soaked rags or paper towels. Leave rags or paper towels on for about one hour before cleaning. Cleans and shines chrome.

Wooden Furniture

2 parts olive or vegetable oil

1 part lemon juice

Apply mixture to furniture with a soft cloth and wipe dry.

Gold & Silver

Use toothpaste and a soft toothbrush or cloth to clean tarnish from gold and sterling silver (not silver plate). Rinse with clean, warm water and buff dry.

Shoes

Shine shoe leather by polishing it with the inside of a banana peel; then buff with a soft cloth.

Stainless Steel

Use vinegar to remove spots and mineral oil to shine.

In the Laundry

Bleach

Use one cup lemon juice in a gallon bucket half-filled with water, and soak the item overnight. Or, substitute one-half cup borax per wash load to whiten whites and brighten colors.

Detergent

Detergents were designed to clean synthetic fibers. Natural fibers clean up quite adequately with natural substances. Use borax, baking soda, washing soda, or natural soap instead of detergent. A good mix is equal parts borax and washing soda. If you live in a hard-water area you may have to add a bit more soda.

Starch

1 tablespoon cornstarch

1 pint cold water

Dissolve cornstarch in water. Place the solution in a spray bottle. Shake it before using.

Fabric Softener

Put a half cup vinegar into the final rinse.

Fresheners

Air

Open a box of baking soda in the room.

Carpet

To deodorize carpet, sprinkle baking soda on carpet before vacuuming.

Garbage Disposal

Grind a used lemon or orange in the disposal.

Sachets

Make a simple sachet of dried southernwood (an herb, available at botanical centers and health food stores), and store it where you keep woolens.

Instead of mothballs, use cedar chips or sachets of dried lavender.

Stain by Stain

General Stains

Mix one part white distilled vinegar and one part distilled warm water (or ⅓ cup distilled vinegar and ⅔ cup distilled warm water) into a spray bottle. Spray on area, then blot (do not push in stain). Repeat as necessary.

Basin, Tub, Tile

Rub the stain with half a lemon dipped in borax. Rinse, and dry with a soft cloth.

Candle Wax

Use an ice cube to harden the wax, then scrape wax off.

Alternatively, heat an iron to medium setting. Put a paper towel on the wax you want removed and press the iron to it; do not rub. Repeat with clean towels until wax is gone.

Coffee

Blot with club soda.

Grease

Rub a grease spot with damp cloth dipped in borax. Or, apply a paste of corn-starch and water; let it dry and brush it off.

Gum

Use an ice cube to harden, then scrape if off.

Ink

Put cream of tartar on the stain and squeeze a few drops of lemon juice on it. Rub into the stain for a minute, brush off the powder, and sponge with warm water or launder.

Mildew

½ cup vinegar

½ cup borax

warm water

Dissolve vinegar and borax in water, and apply with a clean sponge. Mix fresh for each use.

Oil

Rub white chalk into the stain before washing.

Scorch Marks

To remove a scorch mark from white linen, cut a raw onion and rub its flat side on the scorched area until the juice is absorbed by the cloth. Let it set, then soak it in cold water for a few hours.

Tar

To remove tar, moisten a cloth with eucalyptus oil and rub clean.

Wine

Blot with club soda. To remove red wine, dab out excess moisture with an absorbent cloth and sprinkle salt on the stain. Let it set several hours. When it's dry, brush or vacuum it away. Or, clean the stain immediately with club soda.

A Healthy Home Has…

- Healthy cleaners, not harsh chemical cleaners.

- Household cleaners and chemicals sealed, labeled, and stored in a cool, dry place (not under the sink), in their original containers, and out of reach of children and pets.

- A clean kitchen.

- A clean workshop and basement with no open, half-empty cans of paints, solvents, or cleaners.

- Work gloves available for protecting hands when using irritating cleansers.

- Strict rules for following the EPA's guidelines for proper disposal of hazardous waste.

PESTS

America is a culture of quick-fix solutions, and that includes problems with pests. If ants, moths, fleas, mice, or any number of other pests invade your home, there's a product to buy or a service to hire that can eliminate the problem with harsh synthetic pesticides. Shelves in hardware, grocery, and home improvement stores groan with bottles and sprays developed to rid your house of pests. Unfortunately, most are not safe for human health in the long run.

When it comes to household pests, you need to make an important distinction. While insects are pests, a pest isn't necessarily an insect. Consequently, the terms "pesticide" and "insecticide" are not interchangeable.

Regardless of what you're dealing with, preventing household infestation is key. The best solution is to create conditions that make your home inaccessible and inhospitable to pests in the first place. If you're vigilant and learn to spot signs pests leave behind, you'll notice problems sooner and be able to remedy them with easy, less toxic methods.

Develop a New Philosophy

Instead of getting rid of each and every pest you find, learn how to co-exist with them. First identify what they are. Then make an educated choice about those that can be tolerated and those that cannot.

Admit you don't have to control all pests. Determine what is important, why it is important, and whether you can live with a certain pest or not. Think about picking up those that aren't a health hazard and placing them outside. For example, lady beetles can be a nuisance but they aren't a health hazard. Simply vacuuming them up off the window sill and depositing them outside is vastly preferable to spraying harsh chemicals inside your house.

The Politics of Pesticides

During World War II, the United States began developing, registering, and using a large number of insecticides. Prominent among them was DDT, which was applied both inside and outside the home for years. The U.S. banned DDT when it was discovered that, when exposed, birds and mammals did not excrete the chemical; instead it accumulated in body fat and caused disease. Several species, like the bald eagle, became endangered due in large part to DDT exposure. Pesticides like DDT are sometimes removed from usage when scientific studies prove continued use poses unacceptable risks to people, the environment, wildlife, or applicators; but this takes years, and the damage done in the meantime is considerable.

Fortunately, the days of highly toxic pesticides like DDT, chlordane, and lindane have come and gone. In general, the present generation of commercial pesticides are much less toxic. Still, dangers persist and consumers need to be aware.

Manufacturers spend fortunes lobbying Congress for less restrictive legislation; thus a product may stay on the market long after studies have shown it's harmful to human health. Just because a product is sold doesn't ensure it won't present a hazard. It's up to you, the consumer, to educate yourself on pesticide safety.

Always use nonchemical pest control methods (such as good home hygiene, sealing entry points for pests, and removing sources of food and water) before resorting to synthetic chemicals. If you must use commercial pesticides indoors, ventilate the area well. Store pesticides in original containers in a secure site outside the house, away from people, animals, and in locations not accessible to children. Consult the label to determine active ingredients and signal words.

Inspect the Perimeter

Many pests enter the house through cracks, crevices, seams, and holes in the house structure itself. Go outside and inspect the perimeter. Start with the foundation; then inspect the siding, windows and doors, and finish at the roof. Look for any place a small critter could squeeze through. A crack need only be a fraction of an inch for a cockroach, for example. Mice only need a hole the size of a nickel. Especially check places where utility pipes and wires enter the house, flashing around the chimney, and weatherstripping under doors.

If you find cracks and crevices, fill them with no-VOC caulk or some other form of sealer, but first make sure the edges of the space being sealed are clean and dry. Smooth the caulk so it forms a tight seal and use enough to fill the width of the space and about one-quarter-inch deep. For spaces greater

than one-quarter inch deep, consider using foam fillers and caulk over the foam. Inspect these places occasionally to make sure the filler is holding.

Pests can also enter through holes in screen doors, tiny cracks in the eaves, and through attic vents. Inspect these places, too, and tighten any that may be sources of entry. Protect attic vents with screens.

Eliminate wood-to-ground contact, such as where landscaping has moved soil or mulch up against wood siding. Remove clutter from around the house perimeter, including piles of leaves. Clip back tree limbs and vegetation touching the roof or siding. Stack firewood away from the foundation and elevate it off the ground. Also, eliminate standing water (pools, bird baths, etc.) located within six yards of the house. Keep garbage in a tightly sealed container stored at least ten yards from the house, as well.

Pesticide Health Effects

Pesticides are designed to attack living cells and harm them until the whole organism dies. Pesticides are designed so that small concentrations of lethal chemicals can be directed at a specific target—an insect or a rat in your basement, for example. This design breaks down when you look at the big picture. Approximately 90 percent of all U.S. households use synthetic pesticides. In 2001, 888 million pounds of conventional pesticides were used in the United States, according to EPA figures. Seventy-eight million U.S. households store the stuff in their houses and garages. The aggregate effect of all those targeted, small concentrations is a very diffuse, large concentration.

People are exposed to pesticides primarily in the home. Studies show that the number and concentration of pesticides detected in indoor air are typically greater than those for outdoor air. Conventional pesticides pollute indoor air through indoor use and storage, people and pets tracking in from outdoors, or small amounts of drift during outdoor application. Pesticides may be found indoors even when there is no known use of pesticides on the property. Levels vary from room to room, even within different spots inside the same room. Airborne pesticides settle onto surfaces where they may stay for days or weeks or be resuspended into the air. People are exposed to pesticides by inhaling them (the major route of exposure), accidentally eating them, and getting them on their skin. Building characteristics influence pesticide levels indoors. If the house is leaky, there is more air exchange, so indoor levels decrease. Opening windows and using fans to ventilate helps reduce indoor air pollution levels. Of course, if pesticides are entering the home from outdoor sources, you must minimize the amount of outside air getting in. For example, if there's spraying going on in the neighborhood, close windows and shut off mechanical systems that mix indoor and outdoor air.

An odor is evidence of exposure, though pesticide levels may be found with no odor at all. If you suspect pesticides may be polluting the air inside your house, have it tested. To locate a qualified, commercial laboratory, call the National Pesticide Information Center (see page 170).

Natural & Less-Toxic Remedies

In addition to synthetic pesticides, there is a whole host of natural chemicals that are irritating or fatal to common household pests. In the pages that follow, you'll find information on several of these substances, including how to use them and what pests they affect.

If you find yourself with a pest problem, the healthiest approach may require several steps. Educate yourself on all treatment options and choose the safest one—in application, ingredients, and method—first. Try choosing the natural alternatives listed below before resorting to synthetic chemicals. For severe infestations, you may have to choose a moderately toxic synthetic method. In any case, it's important to know as much about the pest you're dealing with as possible (see pages 85 to 97 for details on common pests) before you put out the poisons. Then, weigh the consequences, know what you are doing, and only buy as much as you need.

Growth Regulators

Instead of using harsh chemicals, consider insect growth regulators, chemicals that aren't harmful to humans but that transform insects into tiny Peter Pans— they eventually die of old age, but they never grow up. Growth regulators are not poisons; they simply stop insects from growing. Two commonly used insect growth regulators are methoprene and fenoxycarb; look for these in the list of active ingredients in the fine print on the label.

Boric Acid

Boric acid clings to insects; when pests clean themselves they ingest it and die after about a week. To use, buy 99 percent technical boric acid powder and sprinkle it in cracks and crevices out of the reach of people and pets. Protect yourself with a dust mask and gloves. Boric acid is effective for six months to a year, depending on your climate. It appears that insects, including roaches, never become immune to it.

When used properly, boric acid is a reasonably safe, effective method of pest control, but it is potentially harmful to humans—just a tablespoon can kill a child. If you use boric acid, follow label directions, seal containers, and keep them out of the reach of children and pets.

Desiccating Dust

Desiccating dust (also referred to as diatomaceous earth or silica aerogel) is another option for dealing with insects. In insects, it causes loss of body fluids and death by dehydration. Desiccating dust is applied to cracks and crevices. Wear a mask and gloves during application. When used as an insecticide, it should be gar-

den- or food-grade (not swimming pool-grade) and, like boric acid, should be kept out of the reach of children and pets.

Pyrethrum Powder

Pyrethrum powder is made from dried and ground-up pyrethrum flowers. It is also a contact nerve poison. It stuns insects, paralyzes their nervous system, and kills on direct contact. The powder itself is only effective for about a day, so there are no worries of the poison lingering. It does, however, cause allergies in some people. Pyrethrum is often combined with more dangerous pesticides, so read the label carefully if you are buying an over-the-counter product.

Common Pests

It's important to know exactly what type of pest you're dealing with so you can apply the most effective and most healthy solution right away, instead of taking a trial-and-error approach that may add unnecessary poisons to your environment.

A few natural chemicals are generally all you need to deal effectively with common pests. Keep growth regulator (a), boric acid (b), desiccating dust (c), and pyrethrum powder (d) in a locked cabinet.

It also helps to remember that pests, too, have a reason for being. A majority of them are harmless or beneficial to humanity. We should try to share our planet with them and live in harmony as best we can.

Ants

Ants, the most prevalent household pest, are close relatives of bees and wasps. They are a health concern for what they track into the house, and can be destructive of the structure. Once ants have established a colony inside or near a building, they may be difficult to control, so prevention is your best bet. If you want to prevent an invasion of ants, avoid pesticides that cause ant colonies to disperse into multiple locations.

Some ants come from outdoors, some nest indoors. Nests are often found next to buildings, along sidewalks, or in proximity to food sources such as trees or plants. They also construct nests under boards, stones, tree stumps or plants, and sometimes under buildings or in wall voids, under flooring, or near hot water pipes or heating systems. Most ants you see are foraging workers; killing them is unlikely to destroy the colony. The queen needs to be destroyed in order to destroy the colony.

Prevention

- Caulk cracks and crevices around the foundation that provide entry from the outside.
- Eliminate cracks and crevices wherever possible indoors, especially in kitchens and other food-preparation and storage areas.
- Store attractive food items such as sugar, syrup, honey, and other sweets in clean, closed containers. Rinse out empty soft drink containers.
- Thoroughly clean up grease and spills.
- Do not store garbage indoors.
- Wipe kitchen countertops daily.
- Keep branches and other vegetation from brushing against your house.
- Don't leave pet food out; if you do, insert the food dish in a bowl of soapy water to prevent ants from reaching it.

Mechanical Pest Control

When getting rid of pests of all kinds, consider old-fashioned mechanical means. Flyswatters and window screens may replace fly sprays. A well-aimed stream of water from a garden hose may replace garden sprays. Careful sanitation may replace cockroach and rodent pesticides.

Don't waste money on so-called ultrasonic pest eliminators. These small electronic units claim to bombard your home with silent sound that turns roaches and other pests into nervous wrecks and makes them vacate the premises. Pests appear to become conditioned to the sound quickly, so the devices have no observable effect. Don't use electrical devices, either, as a means of getting rid of flying insects. They're unsettlingly noisy, and the light attracts insects instead of repelling them.

Control

- Frequent reapplication of sticky barriers sometimes prevents ants from crawling up foundation walls or table legs.
- Garden- or food-grade desiccating dusts kills ants; always follow label directions.
- Boric acid ant baits may be effective, but use with caution and always follow label directions. Ants will not eat bait if more desirable food is nearby, so remove any particles of food from around sinks, pantries, and other ant-infested areas. Place bait stations in places where ants can easily find them, but avoid placing them in areas that are accessible to small children and pets. Place baits where there are ant trails or along edges where ants travel.

Bed Bugs

Bed bugs are still a problem in some parts of the United States. They are an oval-bodied insect, ¼ to ⅜ inch long when not engorged, brown to red-brown in color, wingless and flattened top to bottom. They feed on blood, mostly from people and usually at night. The bites are irritating, itchy, and noticeable to the eye. Where infestations are severe, you may detect an offensive odor that comes from an oily liquid the bugs emit. Bugs feed regularly when temperatures are above 70 degrees F.

Prevention

The only preventive is careful management—find places where bed bugs hide in the daytime and clean those sites as thoroughly as possible. Look for black or brown spots around the seams, tufts or fold of mattresses and daybed covers. In severe infestations, they may be found behind baseboards, window and door casings, loosened wallpaper, pictures and picture frames, and in furniture and cracks in plaster.

Control

- Focus on mechanical methods, such as vacuuming and removing or sealing loose wall surfaces, such as wallpaper and paint.
- Caulk cracks, crevices, and other hiding places.
- Vacuum the mattress, paying attention to tucks and along seams. Remove and seal the vacuum cleaner bag immediately after cleaning. Place the bag into a plastic garbage bag, tightly seal, and discard.
- Thoroughly clean the slats, springs, and frame of the bed.
- Steam cleaning probably does not help because the mattress quickly absorbs heat and bedbugs are not harmed.
- Encase the mattress in a zippered cover, such as those used for dust mites. Bed bugs can live a long time without a meal, so leave the mattress cover on for at least a year.
- After thoroughly cleaning, move the bed away from the wall.
- Coat the bed legs for three to four inches with petroleum jelly to prevent bugs from crawling up into the bed.
- Keep bed covers and blankets off the floor.

Carpet Beetles

Carpet beetles are destructive and may cause allergies. Adults lay eggs in furs, woolen fabrics, carpets, stuffed animals, leather book bindings, feathers, silk, natural bristle hair brushes, dried plant products, and occasionally spices and grains.

Larvae shed skins and fecal pellets, which are about the size of a grain of salt, making it obvious where they are nesting. Adults usually appear in spring or early summer and are often seen indoors near windows. They feed on flowers and may be brought into the home in bouquets. Carpet beetles are among the most difficult indoor pests to control. For that reason, it's best to stop them before they enter the house.

It is not always possible to tell if damage is caused by clothes moths or carpet beetles, but in general, beetles are more likely to damage a large area on one portion of a garment or carpet while moth damage more often appears as scattered holes.

Prevention

- Keep carpets lint-free and inspect clothing for infestation.
- Store woolens in airtight garment bags or plastic containers.
- Do not leave windows open in the spring unless they are covered with tight-fitting screens.
- Caulk all cracks in the siding or eaves, and screen attic vents. Seal cracks along interior moldings and the openings around pipes and heating vents.
- Examine cut flowers for adult beetles.
- Protect fabrics by keeping them clean. Food and perspiration stains attract carpet beetles.
- Inspect stored textiles. Air, brush, and hang them in the light on a yearly basis. If infestations are found, launder or wet-clean before returning them to storage.

Control

- The best control is regular and thorough cleaning of rugs, draperies, upholstered furniture, closets, and other locations where carpet beetles are found.
- Frequent, thorough vacuuming is an effective way of removing food sources as well as eggs, larvae, and adults. After vacuuming infested areas, dispose of the bag promptly.
- If you find beetles in foodstuffs, freezing infested items for forty-eight hours should take care of them.
- Some furniture, mattresses, and pillows are stuffed with hair or feathers. If carpet beetles get into the stuffing, the only sure way to eliminate them is to have the infested item treated with lethal gas in a fumigation vault. Best to just get rid of the infested item.
- Sticky traps baited with an appropriate pheromone can show where beetles are coming from. Sticky traps are also available without a pheromone; these can be placed on window sills to trap adults that fly to windows.
- Borate insecticides in dust formulations are a moderately toxic remedy, effective when fumigation is needed and infestations are extensive.

Carpenter Ants

Like termites, carpenter ants destroy wood inside the home. These insects vary in size and color but are usually large (¼ to ½ inch) and black. Occasionally, swarms of winged carpenter ants emerge into a home. Swarms usually occur in the spring and are a sure sign a colony is nesting somewhere inside the structure.

If you find wood damaged with smooth, clean galleries and dump piles resembling sawdust, it's a sign of infestation. They typically choose water-damaged wood, insulation, or voids for nesting. Consequently, nests are likely to be found in and around sinks, bathtubs, poorly sealed windows and door frames, roof leaks, and poorly flashed chimneys.

No matter what control method is used, you must first locate and expose the nesting area. Since there often is no sign of external damage, locate hidden nests by probing the wood with a screwdriver to reveal the excavated galleries. Or, tap along baseboards of other wood surfaces with the blunt end of a screwdriver, listening for the hollow sound of damaged wood. If a nest is nearby, carpenter ants often respond by making a rustling sound, similar to the crinkling of cellophane.

Carpenter ants may have parent or satellite colonies outside the house. To rid your house of infestation you must also get rid of these satellite colonies. Find the outdoor colonies by feeding indoor ants small dabs of diluted honey placed onto the nonsticky side of masking tape. Do this late at night since that is when the ants are most active. After the ants have fed on the honey, follow them back to their nest. Be patient; they will eventually disappear behind a baseboard, cabinet, into a wall, door casing, or porch column.

The extent and potential damage depends on how many nests are present and how long the infestation has been active. Although large carpenter ant colonies are capable of causing structural damage, it is usually not as serious as damage caused by termites.

Prevention
- Correct roof leaks, plumbing leaks, and other moisture problems and provide adequate ventilation.
- Replace water-damaged wood.

- In moisture-prone areas, use naturally water-resistant wood such as redwood or western red cedar.
- Continually monitor for signs of infestation.

This is a carpenter ants' nest. Carpenter ants typically attack water-damaged wood, so controlling moisture is critical to preventing infestation.

Control
- Treat wall voids and other hidden spaces where ants are entering by carefully drilling a series of small ⅛ inch holes and puffing boric acid into suspected nest areas. If you suspect the nest is in a wall, drill and treat at least 3 to 6 feet on either side of where ants are entering. Use caution, though. Never insert metal-tipped devices around electrical outlets.
- Desiccating dust may also help; follow label directions.

Centipedes & Millipedes

Centipedes and millipedes can wander into the house from the garden. They resemble worms and provide harmless and beneficial natural insect control outdoors. They do no damage indoors and pose no health hazard. When disturbed, millipedes do not bite, but some species exude a defensive liquid that can irritate skin or burn the eyes. When provoked, a few large kinds of centipedes can inflict a painful bite that may cause localized swelling, discoloration, and numbness.

Prevention
- Eliminate holes in screens and cracks in walls and other openings.
- Reduce moisture and air out damp places.
- Remove rotting wood and decaying grass and leaves from around the house foundation.

Control
- Capture and release outside.

Clothes Moths

Like carpet beetles, clothes moths eat items made of wool, hair, or feathers. This includes clothing, blankets, quilts and pillows, felt keys on pianos, old felt insulation, and stuffed toys. Close examination of an infested object reveals the presence of silken webs that are spun by the larvae. Clothes moths may enter your house on rodents, birds, or other insects.

Prevention
- Frequently used items are safe from moth damage, but stored items should be carefully washed or wet-cleaned before storage, or hang them outside in the sun. Pay special attention to pockets, collars, pleats, and seams.
- Store items in airtight containers in a cool, dry location. A closet or room is better than an attic or basement.
- Keep window and door screens in good condition.

- Seal cracks and crevices around baseboards, doors, and windows.
- Check stored items regularly for infestation.
- Vacuum piano felts frequently.

Control
- Heat an infested object for at least 30 minutes at temperatures over 120 degrees F, or freeze the object for several days at temperatures below 18 degrees F, or fumigate with dry ice.
- Use herbal sachets in a drawer with woolen items that you use only occasionally. Natural repellants include dried lavender, cedar chips, tobacco leaves, pennyroyal leaves and stems, dried southernwood, and pyrethrum daisy flowers. Remember to give sachets a little squeeze from time to time to release a fresh burst of scent.
- Store items in airtight cedar chests. Lightly sand the wood inside to release more scent.
- Place pheromone traps to help reduce infestations in closets and other areas where clothes are stored.

Cockroaches

Cockroaches have been around for millions of years, and will probably be around long after humankind is extinct. While they probably aren't capable of spreading serious disease, their feces are a common allergen.

Cockroaches breed incredibly quickly year-round, and will eat almost anything. Though they can exist in practically any environment—from moist to dry, warm to cool—they prefer dark, crowded spaces with surfaces touching them all around.

These insects are typically found where living conditions resemble their native tropical habitat, typically dark, closed-in spaces.

Prevention

- Repair holes or openings in ducts, windows, pipes, doors, and fixtures with low-VOC caulk.
- Rid your home of newspaper and magazine piles, and keep wood away from exterior walls.
- Get rid of excess moisture. Fix leaky faucets and pipes. Dry out wet dishrags and leave wet sponges in the open air to dry. Regularly empty and clean the drip pan under the refrigerator.
- Exercise good kitchen hygiene. Wash dishes after every meal; keep garbage in tightly sealed containers; clean floors, stovetop, and countertop regularly, especially before bedtime.
- Store food in tightly sealed containers.
- Clean up your pet's food bowl and don't allow pet food to sit out all day.

Control

- Reduce a population of roaches by eliminating its food, water, and shelter.
- Like many other pests, roaches learn to avoid locations treated with chemical pesticides they can smell, and they've become immune to many pesticides.
- Dust boric acid powder into cracks along baseboards and moldings, underneath and behind stoves and refrigerators, around plumbing fixtures, underneath kitchen and bathroom cabinets, and into openings in the walls. Studies show applying boric acid to roach hiding places provides 99 percent roach control for three months.
- Apply desiccating dust in the same way as boric acid.
- Use insect growth regulators, pyrethrum, homemade baited traps, and commercial traps.

Fleas

Fleas are probably the most annoying insect in the home. They live off the blood of a warm-blooded host. Flea bites are itchy and annoying. Some people and pets develop an allergy to flea bites that can cause irritation for weeks.

Fleas thrive in warm, humid weather and have four life stages: egg, larva, cocoon, and adult. Eggs are laid on the host animal; when they hatch, larvae drop onto surfaces in the home—carpet, blankets, furniture—and live by feeding on adult flea droppings, eventually becoming adults when they find a host.

You can evaluate a flea problem in your house by wearing knee-high white socks and walking around your home and yard. Dark colored fleas are clearly visible when they jump on white socks. Check your socks often so you know which areas have the most fleas.

Chemical flea collars, dips, and sprays may be more harmful to your pets than the fleas themselves.

Prevention

- Keep pets in good health—well-fed, well-exercised, and well-loved.
- Bathe pets regularly; groom with a flea comb.
- Thoroughly and regularly vacuum your home to remove eggs, larvae, pupae, and adult fleas.
- Keep your pet's bedding clean.
- Add brewer's yeast or garlic to your pet's diet; carefully follow the label for proper dosage.

Control

- Frequently empty your vacuum cleaner bag, which can be a reservoir of fleas, and remove from the house immediately.
- Steam clean and wash floor coverings.

- Comb pets with a flea comb daily to monitor the size of the population. Flick fleas into a bowl of soapy water to kill them.
- Use a nontoxic flea shampoo such as Earthbath, PetGuard, or Safer Flea Soap weekly or monthly, depending on the size of the population. Citrus shampoo is also useful, but read the label carefully for ingredients.
- If a professional exterminator is called, ask for a nontoxic method, such as borate salt forced deep into carpets. Though it takes two to six weeks to completely destroy an existing flea population, it is guaranteed to continue working for a year.

House Flies

These are the most common type of fly found around the home. Besides being fast and proficient breeders, house flies are known to carry over 100 different kinds of disease-causing germs. They taste with their feet, which are 10 million times more sensitive to sugar than the human tongue. They're drawn to bright light and feed on decomposing material.

Prevention
- Use fine mesh screens on windows and doors; quickly repair holes.
- Keep garbage tightly sealed and remove trash regularly.
- Clean up regularly after your pet.
- If you maintain a compost pile, turn it frequently.

Control
- Try using a good old-fashioned fly swatter.
- Fly traps (which attract flies with a pheromone) are widely available and effective.

Mice

Found in all fifty states, the house mouse is the most common rodent pest. It breeds rapidly and throughout the year, quickly adapting to changing conditions. Mice live both indoors and outdoors, and can share nests. House mice are not benign. They bring fleas, mites, ticks, and lice into the house, and even a tiny droplet of their urine can cause an allergic reaction in children. Hantavirus pulmonary syndrome (HPS) is a deadly disease transmitted by infected rodents through urine, droppings, or saliva. Humans can contract the disease when they breathe in aerosolized virus. When cleaning up mouse droppings or nesting materials, moisten the area first with a water sprayer, then wear gloves and a respirator to reduce your risk of contamination.

The easiest way to prevent mice from entering your home is to eliminate hiding places. Unfortunately, if you live in a cold-weather climate, you may notice an influx when seasons change as mice seek cover from the cold.

Prevention
- Mice can squeeze through spaces as small as a nickel, so seal all holes, gaps, or cracks in your home's structure that are larger in diameter than a pencil.
- Keep woodpiles twelve inches off the ground and away from the house.
- Keep vegetation from touching the exterior of your house.
- Store all trash in sealed containers.
- Make sure gutters channel water away from the house.
- Lightly sprinkle flour where you suspect mice are finding their way into your home; their tracks in the flour will point to their entry point.

Control

- Use catch-and-release, snap, or glue traps. Position snap traps at right angles to walls with bait towards the walls. Check all traps daily.
- Use toxic commercial pesticides only as a last resort.

Mosquitoes

A mosquito bite causes severe skin irritation resulting in a red bump and uncomfortable itching. More seriously, mosquitoes transmit diseases like malaria, dengue fever, encephalitis, and West Nile virus. There are about 200 different species of mosquitoes in the U.S., all sharing common traits. Most lay eggs in standing water. Contact your local mosquito control district or health department if you have any questions about mosquitoes and their control in your neighborhood.

The flowing water of rivers and streams helps keep these bodies of water free of mosquito larvae, but marshes, swamps, clogged ditches, and temporary pools and puddles are prolific breeding sites. Other wet outdoor breeding sites include tree holes, old tires, buckets, toys, potted plant trays, saucers, and plastic covers.

Prevention

- Dump out and drain any standing water in your yard.
- Keep window and door screens in good shape.
- Empty and change water in birdbaths, fountains, wading pools, rain barrels, and potted plant trays at least once a week.
- Keep swimming pools treated and rain gutters unclogged.
- If there is a mosquito-borne disease warning in effect, stay inside during the evening when mosquitoes are most active.

- Replace outdoor lights with yellow "bug" lights.

Control

- Stock ponds with mosquito larvae-eating fish.
- Use nontoxic repellants, such as Avon's Skin-So-Soft lotion, and wear long sleeves to decrease the number of mosquito bites over a short period of time.

Pantry Pests

Several insects infest food stored in the kitchen and pantry. They include meal moths, various beetles, weevils, and mites. Some enter from outdoors but, more likely, they enter the home in grocery bags. You may notice clumps of food clinging to the sides of a container or find soft web-like cocoons in your food. Sometimes, adult moths will fly away when you open a container.

Prevention

- Carefully inspect every package containing dried food coming into the house—flour, crackers, peas, pasta, fruit, nuts, flowers, herbs, spices, pet food. Look for tiny holes or loose cardboard flaps.
- If a package is leaking, it may already be contaminated. Take it back to the store. Don't keep it in your cupboard or pantry as the infestation will spread to other food.
- Buy what you need when you need it instead of storing dry food for long periods of time.
- Keep pantry shelves clean and dry.
- Store food in tightly sealed containers.
- Don't combine old foods with new.
- Check stored foods regularly for contamination and throw out anything that looks suspicious.

Control

- Kill pests by placing the food in a sealed bag and putting it in the freezer for two days.

- Heat kills some pantry pests. Spread dry food thinly on cookie sheets and heat to 125 degrees F for two hours. Cool food completely before repackaging.
- Large amounts of grain can be protected by thoroughly mixing it with diatomaceous earth. Use one cup of food-grade diatomaceous earth for every 25 pounds of grain.
- Pheromone traps may catch adult moths before they breed and lay eggs in your food.

Silverfish & Firebrats

Silverfish like to make a meal out of paper, books, cereal, wallpaper paste, and cotton. Silverfish are shiny silver or pearl gray. Firebrats are shiny and mottled gray. Both are slender, wingless, soft-bodied, and $\frac{1}{3}$ to $\frac{1}{2}$ inch long with scaly bodies that taper to the rear. Both species hide during the day and seek food and water at night. They prefer cereals, moist wheat flour, books, paper with glue or paste, sizing in paper (including wallpaper), book bindings, and starch in clothing. They can live for several months without food.

These insects may be brought into the house on lumber, drywall, or similar products. Silverfish live in damp, cool places, like basements and laundry rooms. Firebrats thrive in warm, moist places. Look for them around ovens, furnaces, fireplaces, hot water pipes, and the attic in summer.

Prevention
- Increase ventilation in bathrooms and basements.
- Keep basements, laundry rooms, and bathrooms (especially shower stalls) clean and dry.
- Plug or putty holes or spaces around pipes.
- Repair leaks and drips in plumbing.
- Replace old, peeling wallpaper.
- Store books in a dry location, and periodically move books around in the bookcase.
- Clean out closets occasionally.
- Keep foods in containers with tight lids.

Control
- Kill individual silverfish or firebrats when you spot them.
- Place desiccating dust or boric acid powder close to where the insects reside. Apply a fine layer with a bulb duster, powder blower, or plastic squeeze bottle. Apply directly to cracks in doors and window casings, baseboards, closets, bookcases, and places where pipes go through walls, paying special attention to cracks and crevices. If the dust or powder gets wet, the area must be re-treated.

Spiders

Though there are some poisonous spiders, most species don't harm people. In fact, most are beneficial due to their role as insect predators. Poisonous spiders are limited to specific geographic locations and spend most of their time hidden under furniture or boxes, or in woodpiles, corners, or crevices.

Unlike mosquitoes, spiders do not seek people in order to bite them. In general, they won't bite a person unless they have been squeezed, lain on, or provoked. The severity of a spider bite depends on the kind of spider, the amount of venom injected, and the age and health of the person bitten. A spider bite may cause no reaction, or it may result in itching, redness, stiffness, swelling, and pain similar to that of a bee sting. People vary in their response to a spider bite, however. If a severe reaction occurs, contact a physician, hospital, or poison control center.

Prevention
- Find out what type of spiders are typical to your specific geographic area.
- Remove hiding spots for reclusive spiders such as black widows by regularly cleaning webs with brushes and vacuums.
- Inspect firewood, plants, and boxes before bringing them into the house.
- Regularly vacuum and sweep windows, room corners, storage areas, basements, and other seldom-used areas.
- Seal cracks in the foundation and other parts of the structure, as well as gaps around windows and doors.
- Provide good screening on windows and doors.
- Place boxes off the floor and away from walls in storage areas. Seal boxes with tape.
- Clean up clutter in garages, sheds, basements, and other storage areas. Wear gloves to avoid bites.
- Outdoors, keep areas next to the foundation free of trash, leaf litter, and heavy vegetation.

Control
- Pesticide control is rarely necessary.
- Crush an individual spider with a rolled up newspaper or a shoe.
- For severe infestations, pyrethrins may help. Call a professional.

Termites

All pests can be a nuisance, but termites are in a class of their own when it comes to damaging a home. They cause an estimated $5 billion in structural damage in the U.S. per year. But traditional soil treatments to get rid of termites are almost worse; they pump 300 to 500 gallons of pesticide solution into the ground surrounding your house, a harsh solution.

Dry-wood termites are found across the southern half of United States from California to the East Coast and up the Atlantic seaboard to North Carolina. Damp-wood termites are found in Pacific Coast states and in portions of southern Florida. Each type presents itself differently, and must be treated differently.

Regardless of the type of termite, thorough annual house inspections are important in protecting your home from attack. Slab-on-grade-style buildings are the most susceptible to termite infiltrations. A monolithic-type slab, which slightly thickens at the perimeter, can help.

Before an infestation occurs, monitor your home for the following signs and symptoms of termite damage:
- Pencil-wide mud foraging tubes on foundation walls, piers, sills, joists, etc.
- Winged "swarmer" termites, or their shed wings, on window sills and along the edges of floors.
- Damaged wood hollowed out along the grain, lined with bits of mud or soil.

There is no easy treatment. Often, the control method is not whether to use a chemical treatment, but which chemical treatment to use. Because so much is at stake, treating a house for termites is not a do-it-yourself job. It deserves professional attention. Talk to a professional about moderately toxic alternatives to traditional toxic extermination methods.

Termite nests are easily identifiable by the channels the insects cut. Extensive damage like this calls for immediate action from a professional.

Prevention

- Eliminate wood contact with the ground. Wood siding, latticework, door and window frames, and similar items should be at least six inches above ground level. Regrade or pull soil or mulch back from the foundation. Support steps or posts on a concrete base. Pressure-treated wood is not immune to termite attack.
- Don't allow moisture to accumulate near the foundation.
- Divert water away from the foundation with properly placed gutters, downspouts, and splash blocks.
- Repair or replace leaking faucets, water pipes, and air conditioning units.
- Slope ground away from the foundation so surface water drains away from the building.
- Earthen crawl spaces should be covered with a vapor barrier and sealed at the perimeter.
- Never store firewood, lumber, or wood debris against the foundation or inside a crawl space. Firewood, lumber, cardboard boxes, newspapers, and other cellulose materials attract termites and provide a source of food. Vines, ivy, and other dense plant material touching the house should also be avoided.
- Use mulch sparingly. Because mulch retains moisture, termites are drawn to it, though it is a poor source of food. Crushed stone and pea gravel also attract termites since they retain moisture in the underlying soil.

Control

- An unshielded microwave device raises an infected area's temperature to 190 degrees F, killing dry-wood termites.
- Other treatments tent the house, then raise its temperature to 160 degrees F for four to six hours; however, results need to be closely monitored and there is damage risk for household items, especially plastics.
- Insect growth regulators do an effective job of controlling termites.
- Boric acid is the least toxic termiticide. In new construction, lumber can be pretreated; in older houses, sprays or wood injection will increase resistance to termites.

Wood-Boring Beetles

Wood-boring beetles can enter a house in infested wood that has not been kiln-dried. Infestations are most likely to occur in newly installed wood paneling, molding, window and door frames, plywood, hardwood floors, bamboo products, and furniture, as well as in beams, and foundation timbers. Some species may be found in firewood stored inside; others attack books, still others may bore through plastic, plaster, or soft metal, such as lead and silver.

They leave tiny, round exit holes in

infested wood, and fill galleries with a fine dustlike powder, pellets, or coarse powder that occasionally fall out of exit holes into small piles on the floor or other surfaces. Their life cycle ranges from three months to two years, depending on temperature, humidity, and food source.

Prevention

- Sanitation is imperative. Remove and destroy dead tree limbs around buildings or near any area where wood products are stored. Destroy scrap lumber before it becomes infested.
- Materials used for construction and wood furniture should be thoroughly inspected before use. Look for exit holes where adult beetles have emerged.

- Protect wood from infestation by painting or varnishing to seal pores, cracks, and holes.
- Bring in only enough firewood to burn that day.

Control

- Remove and replace infested structural wood whenever possible. Destroy infested wood by burning it or taking it to a landfill.
- Borate pesticides can potentially kill beetles but must be applied by a licensed pest control operator.

A Healthy Home Has…

- A clean and dry kitchen and bathrooms.

- Food kept in tightly closed containers.

- Tightly sealed garbage containers that are emptied frequently.

- A solid, sealed exterior with no holes or cracks.

- Clearly labeled pesticides, sealed tightly, and stored in their original containers out of reach of children and pets.

- Well-groomed and healthy pets.

Around the Yard

Most people care for their yard with conventional methods, using fertilizers, pesticides and herbicides, and planting trees and plants without thought to water damage, home comfort, or personal risk. The fact is conventional methods expose you and your family to harmful chemicals, as well as unsafe practices. Moreover, people often forget that, though a garage or shed isn't part of a living space, it can affect the health of nearby living spaces. When maintaining a healthy, safe home, include the yard, garden, and all exterior structures, too. Attention to these areas helps protect your house from water damage, insects, noise, and polluted air and water.

Get a Plan

Start by getting a sense of your whole property. Make a drawing on graph paper. Inventory the whole yard, measuring the boundaries, and noting all existing elements. Include your house, garage, and shed (if any); utility poles, deck, patio, fence, trees, and plants. Indicate directionals (north, south, east, west) and take stock of the USDA hardiness zone, light conditions, patterns of shade and wind, as well as dry and wet soil patches.

Make a list of what you want from your healthy landscape. Do you want to grow your own vegetables? Eliminate unsafe chemicals? Shield your house from neighbors? Block noise? Keep moisture from seeping into the foundation? Prioritize your list, and begin with the most pressing issues.

Plant, Shrub, & Tree Selection

Landscape plants add beauty and value to any home, but when carefully chosen with home health in mind, they can also improve quality of life.

Well-chosen, strategically placed trees and other plantings are the most important factors when it comes to controlling wind, sun, shade, heat gain, and glare. They shield your house from wind, reducing surrounding air temperatures and filtering pollutants. In many climates, well-placed trees and shrubs eliminate the need for air conditioning, or at least reduce the number of hours you'll need to have it running. In a temperate climate, work to deflect winter winds. In a hotter climate, allow summer winds to naturally cool the house.

Deciduous trees provide effective energy controls, shading your house in summer, then dropping their leaves so winter's low sun can angle through the windows and warm the house. For the best summer shade, plant trees on the south and west sides of the house. If you live in a climate with harsh winters, tall evergreens on the northwest side provide a natural windbreak to redirect and reduce chilling winds.

No matter the climate, a row of smaller evergreens three to four feet from the northern house wall will act as a layer of insulation. For maximum protection, plant the windbreak a distance from your house two to five times the mature height of the trees. Vines can also shade your house, but never allow them to grow on or penetrate walls, windows, or doors, as they can damage the structure. Train them on trellises, instead. Shade as much of your pavement as possible, and shade your air conditioning unit, taking care to leave airflow unobstructed.

Trees and shrubs can also help block noise and improve privacy. Planting a hedge at the edge of your property provides both a natural fence and a noise filter. Be careful, though, that you don't provide a hiding place for intruders. Well-placed lighting helps, as does keeping the hedgerow a few feet away from the house.

Lawn & Garden

Gardens and flower beds are natural choices for a healthy home. In many regions, cultivating native plants and ground cover is vastly preferable to all the labor, chemicals, and fertilizer required to maintain a "traditional" lawn.

Take care that the landscape and any plantings near the foundation of your house are properly graded. Keep at least one foot of space between the house and full-grown plants, and grade away from the house to divert water. Flower beds that create standing water or that direct water back toward the foundation can contribute to basement moisture, excessive indoor humidity, and, eventually, mold.

If you have a traditional lawn or will be installing one, take the time to cultivate a lawn that won't require excessive watering or chemical fertilizers. Consider grass varieties that grow short and use little water.

Healthy Ways to Care for Your Landscape

Planning and establishing a healthy landscape is only half the battle. All landscaping requires careful and regular maintenance to look its best. A healthy landscape is no different—just make sure your maintenance procedures are as healthy as the landscape. Here are some guidelines.

Healthy Lawn Maintenance

If you have a traditional grass lawn, resist the temptation to make it look like a putting green. Keep it long—from 3 to 3 ½ inches—and mow with a sharp blade. That way, it will be healthier, shade itself, and reduce weeds. Annually removing plugs from the grass with a lawn aerator boosts soil health by adding oxygen and increasing moisture retention.

Leave clippings on the lawn; they are a natural, free fertilizer that won't kill the grass. Do sweep clippings from paved areas to prevent them from entering the water system.

Use your lawn mower as infrequently as possible; it contributes to air pollution. The healthy home has an old-fashioned push mower fueled by elbow grease, not gas. For larger lawns, electric mowers have improved considerably in recent years and are viable alternatives to gas mowers.

Watering

First, measure your natural rainfall with a rain gauge, then supplement only as needed. For example, if you have a built-in irrigation system, don't water on an automatic schedule. Instead, track weekly rainfall and turn the system on so plants receive a total of an inch a week. To measure how long it takes a sprinkler or irrigation system to water the needed amount, set out a can to capture the water. When you do water, make sure to drench only planted areas, not pavement. Soaker hoses and drip irrigation (small tubes snaked around plants that slowly release water) are good choices, getting water directly to plants and preventing evaporation.

Weeds & Pests

Americans annually apply 380 million pounds of herbicides and pesticides classified by the EPA as probable carcinogens. Popular nonselective herbicides, like Roundup, Preen, and others containing diazanon, may contain up to 98 percent "inert" ingredients, which don't have to be listed, meaning you have no idea what is in them. Recent studies indicate that exposure to twenty-six of the most commonly used house and garden formulas increased the risk for non-Hodgkin's lymphoma, brain cancer, and leukemia, especially in children. An EPA study in Florida found the highest household pesticide residues in carpet dust.

Nourishing your lawn naturally cuts down on the amount of additives and herbicides necessary to keep it healthy, and helps plants and trees defend themselves against pests and weeds.

Any synthetic pesticide you use will have unintended consequences and kill beneficial insects, birds, and butterflies. It may not do much good, anyway. Some authorities claim that over half of the insect pest species are now resistant to pesticides due to our massive use of synthetic pesticides.

If you can't control the problem through biological or cultural methods (such as removing a plant that attracts a certain pest), spot treat it, or regulate its growth with the proper application of the safest chemicals possible. Introducing bugs, such as praying mantises, may help control certain problems.

Mulch

Mulch all plants—flowers, vegetables, trees, and shrubs—with two to three inches of organic material (such as wood chips or cedar bark) to enrich the soil, retain moisture, and keep weeds under control. Make certain the mulch is organic, meaning untreated with synthetic chemicals. Mulch once or twice a year, either in spring or fall, and carefully layer the mulch, keeping an inch or two between plant roots and the mulch. When mulching trees, don't create a mulch "volcano" (mulch piled high, then dipping to meet the roots). This can trap moisture and become a habitat for pests. Avoid black plastic; it diverts

Standing Water

Decorative water features are attractive but they can also be a problem. If you want to provide a shallow birdbath or dish with stones for birds or insects, it's best to include a bubbling feature to prevent the water from becoming stagnant. Regularly cleaning the bath keeps it disease-free so birds do not become ill.

moisture and increases heat gain. Don't mulch with rocks, either; they add nothing to enrich the soil.

Fertilizers

If you decide to apply fertilizer to your lawn, make it as organic as possible. Some commercial fertilizers contain poisons like lead, cadmium, mercury, and dioxin, results of toxic waste from steel mills, and paper mills being turned into fertilizer.

Most over-the-counter lawn fertilizers have three numbers on the package, representing levels of nitrogen, phosphorous, and potash. It's a ratio that doesn't take into account whether your plants need those chemicals. Instead, periodically replenish your soil—whether over your lawn or in your garden bed—with organic fertilizer. Organic fertilizer is usually cow manure or compost that you have created. At least once each year, spread an inch or two of compost around plants and trees in your yard. Use a spreader to add compost to your lawn. If you do choose a premix for lawn fertilizer, pick one where the middle number (the phosphorous) is zero, to prevent wasted phosphates from entering the water system.

Compost

A compost pile wins over a garbage disposal hands down when it comes to disposing of organic waste. Garbage disposals require a significant amount of water and load sewage treatment plants and septic tanks with organic matter. Much of what a typical household grinds up in the disposal is compostable. Composting returns organic matter to the earth, improving soil structure and water retention.

Buy a compost bucket with a tight-fitting lid for your kitchen, and chop up

---

Composting 101

- No meat, fish, bones, grease, cheese, or oily matter should be composted. You'll attract bugs and unwanted pests, and the pile will take longer to decompose.
- No weeds from the garden if they are going to seed.
- No feces from carnivorous animals.
- Turn your pile frequently, putting what's on the outside in the middle and allowing air to circulate.
- Keep the pile watered.

---

your scraps so they'll decompose more quickly. Set up your compost pile or bin in a well-drained, sunny spot. Keep it no larger than 5×5 feet so you have space to turn it and to remove the finished product. The rule is three to four parts brown material (leaves, grass clippings, shredded newspapers) to one part green material (egg shells, coffee grounds, fruit peelings). With proper watering, enough air, and a bit of turning, the pile "cooks," or heats up to about 140 degrees F at its core, as microorganisms digest and break down the organic trash into what gardeners call "black gold."

Outdoor Structures

Thoroughly check any outdoor structures for sharp points, broken pieces, or other elements that could cause harm. Make sure tables, grills, and playsets are placed on level ground, and that outdoor structures are solidly built.

Play Structures & Picnic Tables

By far the largest source of arsenic exposure for a majority of Americans is wood treated with chromated copper arsenate (CCA) that was used to construct playground equipment and picnic tables. The arsenic rubs off onto hands and is

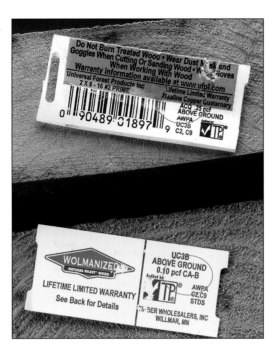

Lumber is labeled with the type of chemical treatment used. If you find a label or a stamp that says "CCA" (above), which stands for chromated copper arsenate, the board contains arsenic. If you need to purchase new treated lumber, look for "ACQ" (upper right) which stands for ammoniacal copper quaternary, or "CBA" or "CA-B" (lower right) both of which stand for "copper boron azole."

absorbed and ingested, especially when children put their hands in their mouths. Research by the Healthy Building Network found that an area of wood the size of a four-year-old's hand contained an average of 120 times the amount of arsenic allowed by the EPA in a 6-ounce glass of water.

Sandboxes

Do you know where the sand in your child's sandbox came from? Some powdery fine-textured sand contains tremolite asbestos and/or crystalline silica, both known human carcinogens. The healthy sandbox contains washed beach or river sand, which is more granular. Before buying, ask at the store or phone the manufacturer to verify the source. When in doubt, don't buy it.

The Shed

A shed is a perfect place for storing fuels and other hazardous household substances until you can properly dispose of them. Proper disposal is key to prevent them from reaching groundwater and surface water supplies. Purchase only the amount of chemicals and fuel needed, and store them in dry, well-ventilated spaces in their original containers, out of reach of pets and kids. Never dump prod-

How to Test Lumber for Arsenic

Sometimes it's hard to tell whether lumber is pressure treated, and it's impossible to tell by sight if pressure-treated lumber contains arsenic. Fortunately, consumer tests are available and easy to use. Better kits require you to send the sample to a lab for evaluation.

Tape the template to the wood surface you want to test. Wipe the area within the template in an S pattern, applying steady pressure. Remove any splinters from the swab and fold it in half, sample sides in. Wipe the area again, and then remove any splinters and fold the swab in half again.

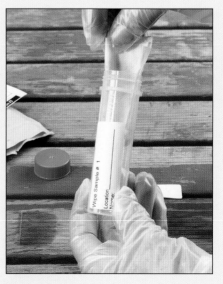

Place the test swab in the plastic vial, fill out the test papers, and send it to the testing company.

ucts in the backyard, down a drain, or toss them in the trash.

Inspect yard equipment and cars regularly for leaking oil, gas, or other fluids. Sprinkle cat litter on spilled fluids; then sweep up with a shovel or broom. Be very careful of spilling antifreeze on the driveway or garage or shed floor. It only takes a teaspoon per pound to poison a dog and even less for a cat.

The Garage

Garages are always safer and healthier when detached from the house. If your garage is attached, tightly seal any windows or doors connecting it to the house to prevent car exhaust and other air pollutants from entering. Try to start engines outside the garage, and don't leave cars running in the garage under any circumstances.

The Driveway

A driveway takes up a substantial portion of an average yard, so it's well worth taking care to choose a healthy material. Asphalt is not an option for a healthy home. It's a proven carcinogen and it emits harmful vapors when installed, and continues to offgas whenever it is heated by the sun. Choose concrete, gravel, or pavers for a driveway, instead.

Dealing with Pressure-Treated Wood

- If wood around your house tests positive for arsenic, follow these guidelines:
- Replace the wood. Many alternatives are now available (see page 102).
- If total replacement is not feasible, consider replacing high-contact areas like handrails on decks and playsets, or the surface deckboards.
- Seal remaining areas at least once a year with a waterproof sealant such as polyurethane or an oil-based penetrating sealer. Test the structure periodically to make sure it is not leaching. Do not use acid deck wash or brighteners, as these accelerate the release of arsenic.
- Never sand or cut arsenic-treated wood. If the wood surface has become rough and splinters are an issue, replace the structure with a less toxic alternative. Splinters from arsenic wood can be dangerous.
- Don't burn arsenic-treated wood. Burning CCA wood creates a highly toxic ash. It should be treated as hazardous waste.
- Always make sure children wash their hands immediately after playing on an arsenic-treated playset and never allow them to eat on a arsenic-treated picnic table without a tablecloth.
- Do not allow children to play in the soil or sand below or around arsenic-treated wood structures. Do not store toys underneath an arsenic-treated structure.
- The soil around and under arsenic-treated wood may contain arsenic, too. You may want to remove this and replace it with uncontaminated soil.

A Healthy Home Has...

- A pesticide-free, herbicide-free yard maintenance program.
- Healthy soil built with organic, homemade compost.
- No CCA pressure-treated wood.

- A detached, locked shed for storing fuel and other hazardous household substances.
- Trees and shrubs to control wind, sun, shade, heat gain, and glare.

HOUSE SYSTEMS

Like the human body, several systems operating together make up the total organism that is a house. Each of these systems needs to be functioning at optimum level for the house to be healthy and efficient.

Heating

Most types of heating systems have a furnace fueled with either electricity or gas. Either fuel is acceptable, though both have drawbacks. The most healthy gas-fired heating system has a sealed combustion chamber—that is, the system gets its combustion air from the outside through one pipe and vents exhaust to the outside through another. If yours is open combustion, be sure it's vented directly outdoors and has a constant supply of fresh air to prevent backdrafting and carbon monoxide problems. Typically, building codes require a

separate fresh-air intake near the furnace. Have your gas system inspected annually.

Electric heat doesn't introduce combustion gases and byproducts into a living space, but it is relatively expensive to run, especially if you live in a cooler climate. It may also present problems associated with electromagnetic fields (EMF). Electric baseboard systems in particular may have high EMFs associated with them.

Distributing Heat

Once a furnace creates heat, a system must deliver it around the house. There are four basic types.

Forced air

This is the most popular type in homes built since the 1950s. It uses a blower to deliver air through a system of ducts to registers around the house. Though not highly energy efficient, this type of system is easy to extend if an addition is built onto the house, and is easily adapted for central air conditioning. This system does have a significant health drawback in that it can, if the ducts aren't regularly inspected and cleaned, circulate air pollution throughout the entire house, provoking health problems for anyone with asthma, allergies, or weakened immune systems.

If you have a forced air system, the single most important thing you can do is keep it maintained. Change the filter regularly and keep ducts and registers clean. If you have a built-in humidifier, make sure you keep it clean and that it is in proper working order.

Hot Water

Systems installed before World War II generally use a boiler to heat water and send it, either through convection or with a pump, to radiators or baseboard convectors throughout the house. Cooled water then returns to the furnace through a return pipe. Most systems installed in the last seventy-five years use pumps, which are more efficient, though more costly to install and repair. Heat is evenly distributed, balanced, and relatively high in humidity.

Since hot-water systems are closed, they can't spread pollutants and cause health problems. They do require regular draining and bleeding of the radiators, however.

Steam

Generally found in houses built before World War II, steam systems work like hot water systems, except they don't need a pump because steam rises vigorously. This type of heat is clean, comfortable, and relatively high in humidity, but radiators tend to get waterlogged, which leads to noise and reduced heat output.

Like hot-water systems, steam radiators don't affect air or water quality, but if they aren't maintained, they can affect your quality of life by making quite a racket. Make sure bleed valves are in working order, and bleed the system whenever a radiator knocks or fails to get hot.

Radiant In-Floor Heat

Radiant in-floor heating systems are increasingly popular—and with good reason; they're efficient, comfortable, and healthy. Radiant systems work like hot-water systems, except, instead of free-standing radiators, hot water runs through tubes embedded in the floor, warming the whole floor and the space above it. Not only is this an option in new construction, it's available as a retrofit. Flooring

Temperature

Generally speaking, optimum indoor temperature is 65 to 68 degrees F. It's easy to get used to overheating (or overcooling), making you vulnerable to colds and sore throats. In most cases, it's better to wrap up more warmly in winter and live in an environment with low background heat. Similarly, in summer it's best to get used to summer's temperatures, relieving them with fans and shade rather than artificial air conditioning.

can be wood, tile, stone, or concrete.

Electrical radiant systems also exist (they uses electrical heating elements embedded in the floor), but hot water is definitely the healthier choice, as most electrical radiant heat generates EMR fields.

Woodstoves & Fireplaces

Fireplaces and woodstoves can be sources of indoor air pollution. The healthiest option is not to have one at all, but if you must, take precautions to protect your home. The best gas fireplaces are sealed combustion models. If you have an older, unsealed model, have the chimney checked and cleaned regularly and install equipment to prevent backdrafting. Keep a carbon monoxide monitor in the same room and open a window slightly to provide fresh air and replenish oxygen levels.

The best wood burning stove is one with a secondary combustion chamber and a catalytic converter. Make sure the stove is carefully installed and have it inspected periodically for leakages. Keep it well maintained for maximum safety.

Austrian and Swedish tiled stoves, made of clay brick or tile with a tiny furnace in the middle, are excellent sources of radiant heat. They use clay or tile as thermal mass, storing heat and radiating it slowly over many hours.

Healthy Forced Air

Unless properly filtered and supplemented with fresh air, forced air systems are a significant source of air pollution. They also produce extremely dry air, which can exacerbate respiratory problems. Remedy the situation by adding a central humidifier to the furnace, or place portable humidifiers in key rooms, such as bedrooms.

Clean Ducts

It's important to have ductwork, registers, and connections professionally checked each year for leaks before the heating season begins. Every year or so, have the ductwork professionally cleaned.

Select the Best Filter

When it comes to air pollutants, there are two kinds: particulates and gases. Each requires a different kind of filter.

Standard cardboard frame filters don't help much when it comes to removing pollutants from indoor air. Their sole purpose is to keep the furnace's fan motor clean.

Medium-efficiency filters are better (and thicker), but may require some minor modifications to the ductwork. They last as long as six months to a year before needing to be changed.

Electrostatic filters and precipitators are also somewhat effective, and can be added to residential furnaces, but they're better at removing smaller particles than large ones, so they require an inexpensive prefilter that must be changed regularly. Still, they may need to be cleaned as often as every week, or every month, depending on how dirty the indoor air is. Plus, many models have the major

How to Install a Forced-Air-System HEPA Filter

Small, portable HEPA (high-efficiency particulate air) filters are good for filtering air in a single room, but for little more than the cost of a couple high-quality portable filters, you can install a HEPA filter in your forced air system. If you're comfortable with aviation snips and sheet-metal screws, you'll have this system up and running in a couple hours.

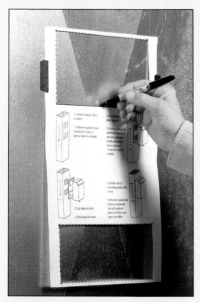

Set your thermostat so the furnace won't run while you're installing the filter. Find the return air duct on your furnace (this is the recommended installation location; consult manufacturer's instructions for alternate locations). Using the mounting plate as a template, mark the two holes on the duct. Cut out the holes using aviation snips. Sheet metal is sharp, so wear gloves.

Position the mounting plate over the holes, and secure it with sheet metal screws. Set the filter on the mounting plate and secure it with the supplied screws. The unit uses a pressure-sensing switch to turn its fan on and off. Make sure the negative pressure tube, located on the back of the unit, is inserted into the return air duct.

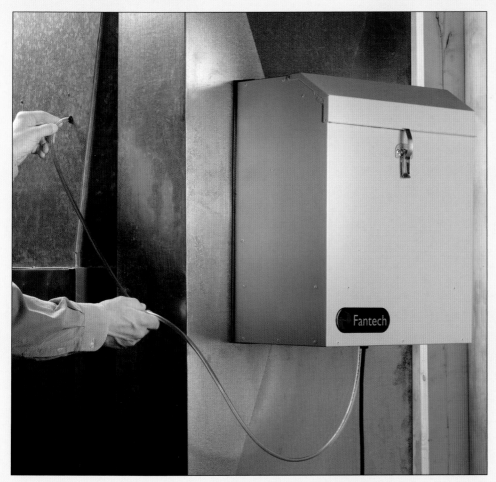

Install the positive pressure tube in the warm air duct. The port for this tube is located on the bottom of the unit. Drill a ¼" hole in the warm-air duct. Carefully file away any burrs, and then insert the rubber grommet into the hole. Insert one end of the plastic tube into the positive pressure port. On the other end, make a mark ½" before the end of the tube. Insert the tube into the rubber grommet so the ½" mark is flush with the grommet. Pull the filters from the unit and remove any packing materials. Replace the filters. Plug the unit into a nearby receptacle or into the furnace's accessory panel. Set the switch to "standby" or "continuous."

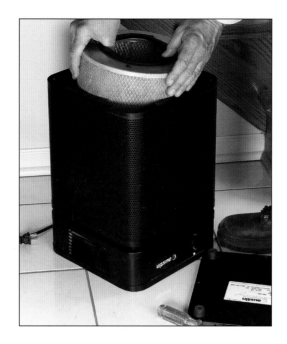

Portable HEPA filters are effective at treating air in rooms. Unlike electrostatic devices, HEPA filters do not produce any ozone. Filters usually need to be replaced frequently.

disadvantage of producing ozone, a known pollutant.

Though it costs more, a high-efficiency particle air (HEPA) filter produces the best results, capturing 99 percent of airborne particulates down to 0.3 microns in size and 100 percent of particulates larger than 1 micron. It is capable of capturing mold spores and most bacteria, as well as construction dust. This also increases the efficiency of air conditioning equipment. A HEPA filter can be added to a residential furnace (see page 107). Portable HEPA filters (ideal for renters) are also available for single rooms. HEPA filters should be changed every six months to a year.

Keep It Clean

Once a week, wipe down the grates on vents on forced air heating systems and make sure the return vent is unobstructed and clean.

Electret or filtrete filters aren't the best at removing particulates, but they aren't the worst, either. They don't produce ozone, and require replacement every four months or so.

Gases are removed from air by a process called adsorption. The filter media most commonly used is activated carbon, which works something like a sponge to remove dozens of gases from the air. Carbon isn't very good at adsorbing formaldehyde, though, the most common gaseous compound found in houses today. For that, activated alumina works best. Some manufacturers mix the two materials to increase filter efficiency.

Cooling

Because a cooling system can be a source of indoor air pollution, and expensive besides, it's important to make it as efficient as possible.

Mechanical Air Conditioning

Mechanical air conditioning isn't used in the healthiest homes. Most indoor air conditioners recirculate indoor air, thereby lowering the rate of indoor-outdoor air exchange, so use them only when absolutely necessary and keep them well maintained. Fresh air is the best conditioner.

A poorly maintained air conditioner can be a source of mold, dust, and disease-causing microorganisms. To prevent this, clean reservoirs regularly with detergent or a hydrogen peroxide solution. If you have a central unit, clean or replace the filters (usually located in the furnace) before the cooling season begins and periodically thereafter. Have the ductwork cleaned regularly. If you have a room unit, clean the filter (located

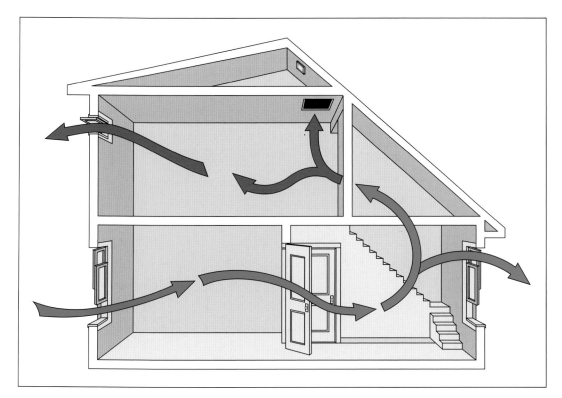

You can facilitate natural cooling with open windows and an attic fan. The whole-house fan (see pages 112 to 113) draws cool air through lower windows and exhausts hot air from the upper story and the attic.

behind the air intake grill on the front) once a month during periods of heavy use. Vacuum dust and lint from the condenser and evaporator yearly.

Natural Cooling

Good insulation and cross ventilation can go a long ways toward reducing or eliminating the need for air conditioning. Before the days of air conditioning, homeowners relied on natural methods for keeping cool. These time-tested methods of old are just as valid today.

- Make sure the attic is adequately ventilated so hot air can escape.
- Plant deciduous trees to shade the south side of the house in summer.
- Install overhangs, awnings, or trellises on the south and west sides to protect windows from the most intense sun.
- Add a screened-in porch on the south or west side to shield the interior of the house from intense sun.

- Block heat with operable shutters.
- Draw fresh air into the house by keeping windows slightly open on the north side.
- Protect living areas from wind and sun with a recessed entry.
- Plant shrubs between the walkway and window to absorb heat reflected from the sidewalk.
- Replace dark-colored roof shingles with light-colored ones.
- Use the porch for social gatherings and sleeping in hot weather.

Humidity

From a health standpoint, the optimum level of indoor relative humidity lies between 40 and 55 percent. It should not fall short of 30 percent and not go beyond 70 percent. This isn't easy to do. Hot, muggy climates have extreme humidity in summer, and cold, dry climates experience too little humidity in winter. A

Condensation Cures

New houses and houses tightened up to conserve energy are the worst for harboring excess humidity. Vapor barriers, storm windows, weatherstripping, and caulking all work to keep moisture inside, which can cause mold to grow, increase VOC offgassing, and lead to deterioration of building materials and furnishings.

The simplest way to remedy the problem is to keep inside air at or below 40 percent relative humidity. Inexpensive, handheld humidity meters are good tools for monitoring the humidity in your home.

If the air is too moist, examine your family's habits to discover where extra moisture is coming from. First, make sure exhaust vents from appliances (like exhaust fans and clothes dryers) are properly installed and leak-free. You can also cut down on excess indoor moisture with small changes like leaving the bathroom vent fan running after bathing (timer switches are available for just this purpose) or cooking with pot lids on whenever possible.

Uncovered crawl spaces may be a big source of excess moisture. Covering yours with 6-mil polyethylene, lapped at least 6 inches at the seams and along the walls, will prevent the moisture from wicking up into the house.

Another solution is to prevent the moisture that does get in the air from entering wall cavities. Plugging cracks, holes, and other openings in your interior walls helps cut down on the amount of air—and therefore moisture—passing into the wall. Painting inside walls with a vapor-barrier paint also helps.

combination of forced-air heating systems and little ventilation can drop humidity levels to as low as 15 percent. Unless you live in an area blessed with constant 50 percent humidity, some moisture will usually have to be added or removed to maintain optimal indoor humidity.

When shopping for a portable humidifier, get the ultrasonic, not the cool-mist kind. Cool-mist humidifiers have a refillable reservoir of water; water molecules are sucked through a filter then blown through air by a fan. Because the water typically sits in the reservoir for long periods of time, these humidifiers become breeding grounds for bacteria. Ultrasonic humidifiers don't breed bacteria as readily. Still, ultrasonic humidifiers pose a risk if run with hard water. Minerals in the water form air-borne dust particles small enough to be inhaled as the mist emitted by the humidifier evaporates. If you have minerals in your water, buy a demineralization filter to remove unwanted particles.

But no matter what kind of humidifier you buy, make sure water doesn't sit in it for long and that it is cleaned daily with hot, soapy water. Do the same with a dehumidifier. Then rinse the tank thoroughly with plain water before refilling.

Ventilation

Excessive moisture, heat, and odors are all forms of indoor air pollution. Some pollutants, like cooking odors, are just unpleasant. But others, like combustion gases, can threaten your health.

Unfortunately, tightening a house to save energy also concentrates pollutants by reducing fresh air that would otherwise leak in through cracks and gaps. The lack of adequate ventilation can cause a host of problems for you and your house.

- Health problems: Accumulated pollutants lead to illnesses, from headaches to lung cancer.
- Moisture damage: Water vapor can condense inside walls and ceilings, leading to mildew, peeling paint, and wood rot.
- Structural damage: Summer sun can heat your attic to 150 degrees F or more; without proper ventilation, this heat can cause roof shingles to deteriorate.
- Higher energy costs: Inadequate attic ventilation also makes your air conditioner work harder.

The solution is not to abandon energy conservation but to attack pollutants at their source. The best way is to bathe the house in fresh air with windows and doors wide open (assuming that outdoor air isn't filled with pollutants such as pollen or industrial smoke). Localized whole-house ventilation (a few open windows combined with a fan in the attic) work to exhaust moist, contaminated air while bringing in fresh air on its heels. It also helps your furnace and air conditioner work more efficiently.

Passive Ventilation

Operable windows and vents in the roof are the critical parts of a passive ventilation system. Make sure your attic is well ventilated. Have an inspector check that existing vents are adequate for the space and are properly installed. You'll want to put vents both high in the ridge and low in the soffit. If that isn't possible, you can put vents in the gable ends.

Encourage passive ventilation by opening leeward windows (located opposite prevailing breezes) more than windward ones. This creates a negative-pressure zone as air moves through the interior of your house, causing more air to exhaust through leeward windows. This, in turn, helps to draw more fresh air into the room. Make sure trees and shrubs are trimmed so they do not block ventilation.

Other passive techniques include:

- Create a *stack effect* by opening windows in the basement or lower level to admit cool air and then opening clerestories, skylights, or dormer windows to exhaust warm air. This works best if the house has an open, central stairway.
- Open windows on opposite sides of rooms. Windows that can "see" each other are three times more effective in creating a cross breeze.

Mechanical Ventilation

Older homes are often leakier than new ones, so they essentially ventilate themselves. Tight houses may require active, mechanical ventilation to control air and moisture.

How much mechanical ventilation do you need? The rule of thumb for the *average* house is a fresh air supply in the range of 100 to 200 cubic feet per minute.

To help your home breathe easier, choose one of the following mechanical ventilation systems:

HOUSE SYSTEMS

How to Install a Timer Switch for a Vent Fan

A vent fan doesn't help much if it can't run long enough, but it only wastes heat and energy if left running too long. The solution is a time-delay switch. A time-delay switch keeps the fan turned on for a preset amount of time and then automatically shuts the fan off. It's easy to replace a standard toggle switch with a time-delay switch.

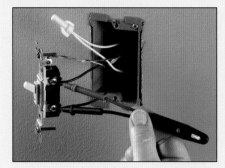

Switch off power to the bathroom at the main circuit breaker panel. Then remove the coverplate from the switch, followed by the mounting screws that hold the switch in place. Carefully pull the switch out of the box, but don't touch any wires. Use a neon tester ($2.99 at any hardware store) to doublecheck that the power is off. Place the probes against the screws on the side of switch (the screws will have black or white wires attached to them). If the tester doesn't glow, it's safe to remove the switch by loosening the two screws that hold the wires in place.

Connect the time-delay switch by connecting the wires you detached from the old switch to the two terminals on the time-delay switch.

Carefully tuck the wires back into the electrical box. Replace the coverplate, and slide the timer knob onto its post. Restore the power and test the switch.

- A network of localized exhaust fans—the least complex system
- A powerful ceiling-mounted whole-house exhaust fan
- A central ventilation system
- An energy recovery ventilator (ERV)—a mechanical system that recovers heat from exhaust air

Exhaust Fans

Localized exhaust fans in the kitchen and bathroom that vent directly outdoors are a minimum requirement in a healthy home.

A kitchen range hood can expel heat, smoke, moisture, and odors—provided it sends the stale air outside. So-called recirculating range hoods don't ventilate at all; their carbon filters remove some odors, smoke, and grease, but they only recirculate moisture and combustion gases.

Bathroom fans help prevent moisture buildup that can lead to mildew and peeling paint. It should provide at least eight air changes per hour. To find the fan capacity you need in CFM (cubic feet per minute), multiply the square footage of the room by 1.1, assuming a standard 8-foot ceiling.

Whole House Fans

A whole-house fan is designed to cool the house during summer by circulating air through all the rooms. A high-powered fan is installed in the ceiling, where it draws in fresh air through windows and pushes out stale air through attic vents. It can lighten your air-conditioning load if you run the fan at night to cool the house and run the air conditioner only during the heat of the day. If outside air temperature is usually below 85 degrees F, a whole-house fan may eliminate the need for an air conditioner altogether.

Whole-house fans usually have thermostats that turn them on when attic air exceeds a preset temperature (typically 90 degrees). Other options include a timer to run the fan at fixed times of day, an insulated cover to stop heat loss through the fan in winter, and a high-temperature safety switch to shut off the fan if the motor overheats.

As with localized ventilation, a whole-house exhaust fan can create negative pressure and cause backdrafting or spillage from combustion appliances. The tighter the house, the more dangerous this can be. For this reason, a tight house requires a balanced system that includes both exhaust and intake of air.

Central Ventilation System

Many houses need mechanical ventilation more in winter than in summer because the windows are closed. A central ventilation system regulates the intake of fresh air and the exhaust of stale air. If you are building a new, airtight house or have extensively caulked and weather-stripped your existing home, this type of system is ideal for you.

Central ventilation uses a single exhaust fan, usually located in the attic. Ducts from the main sources of pollution (kitchens, baths, laundries, workshops) lead to this fan, which discharges pollu-

Warning

Instead of ducting moist bathroom air directly outside, some unscrupulous builders vent it into the attic. This is bad for the house and worth checking on. Look in the attic to make sure the vent's exhaust pipe extends through the roof. If the attic is not accessible, look outside for a roof penetration. Repair improperly vented bathroom fans immediately.

tants outside through a vent.

In an exhaust-only ventilation system only the exhaust is ducted and power vented. Reduced pressure from the ducted air pulls fresh air in through bafflelike one-way intake ports. Unlike an open window, these through-the-wall passages keep out wind and rain. The ports are usually installed in bedrooms and living rooms, preferably where they won't create a draft.

Because cold air is always coming in, the cost of warming it is one drawback to exhaust-only systems (the fan itself is inexpensive to run). If your climate is cold enough and fuel is expensive enough, it makes economic sense to capture heat from the exhaust air and use it to warm the intake air. This is the idea behind the other type of central ventilation, energy recovery ventilators.

Energy Recovery Ventilators

An energy recovery ventilator (ERV) pays for itself most quickly in a tight house in a northern climate. This system has all the advantages of the first type of central ventilation, but it overcomes the problem of cold intake air. When they were first introduced, ERVs were called air-to-air heat exchangers because they let

HOUSE SYSTEMS

the incoming and exhaust air exchange heat without mixing. Today's ERVs work the same way, but they're more efficient, extracting 50 to 80 percent of the heat from the exhaust air.

If you're thinking of buying an ERV, choose a unit that supplies the minimum recommended ventilation rate of 150 CFM. Make sure the manufacturer's ratings of heat-recovery efficiency and airflow capacity are certified by the Home Ventilating Institute (HVI, in the United States) or the Ontario Research Foundation (in Canada). For the most precise control of airflow, look for an ERV with separate blowers for intake and exhaust air.

It's possible to fine-tune an ERV's operating cycle to suit your lifestyle. You can add a humidity control system, if that is needed. Use a timer or a manual override switch to run the ERV when peak indoor pollution is generated—when you are preparing meals or entertaining, for example. And because air is brought in through only one opening and directed through a filter, an ERV helps clean fresh air.

Electrical

Electrical systems can contribute to "sick house" problems in the form of electromagnetic fields (see pages 44 to 45 for more), but safety is the biggest concern when it comes to electricity. Improperly installed, damaged, or outdated wiring and appliances present real fire and shock hazards. If you have an older home and are unsure of the condition of the wiring, it's worthwhile to have a licensed electrician evaluate it. In general, it's good practice to have your wiring inspected every ten years.

Overloaded Circuits

Overloaded circuits are the number one cause of domestic fires. The first step toward electrical fire prevention is to be sure you have adequate capacity for what you're running. Electrical wires are designed to safely carry only so much current. If you exceed that amount by plugging in too many appliances or using too much wattage, you'll trip a circuit breaker or blow a fuse. Fuses and circuit breakers are safety devices designed to prevent circuit overload. If they fail, or don't work quickly enough, more current flows through the wire than the wire can handle, resulting in fire. If you find yourself tripping breakers or blowing fuses regularly on the same circuit, or if the lights dim whenever you run an appliance, don't ignore the problem. Call an electrician to update that circuit.

Protect Against Shock

Water and electricity don't mix. Advances in electrical safety—the three-wire ground system, polarized plugs, double insulation, and ground-fault circuit interrupters (GFCIs)—have decreased the number of accidents involving water and electricity, but the danger is still there, and carelessness is usually the cause. It's up to you to be responsible for safety.

When you buy an appliance destined for use in wet areas, be sure to read the instructions that come with it. Follow those instructions to the letter, and see that others in the house know the dangers. Pay special attention to hair dryers, as they account for 60 percent of all bathtub electrocutions. Unplug them when you aren't actively using them. Even with the switch off, a plugged-in dryer still carries a current.

In the kitchen, don't touch the toaster, mixer, or coffee maker with one hand while you turn on the faucet with the other. Also get into the habit of disconnecting appliance cords at wall receptacles—not at the appliance. A cord removed from an appliance and left plugged into an outlet is energized and could be deadly if it falls into a sink full of water.

Keep spills wiped up in the laundry room. And be wary of a flooded basement. Don't venture into one unless you are positive the water is not in contact with a source of electricity.

EMR

In the home, magnetic fields are produced by wiring when that wiring is not balanced. These not only present health risks, they're actually a violation of building code. The problem is *net current.* Any time you have net current, it shows the wiring is unbalanced, the wires end up getting hot, and a fire hazard exists. The hotter the wires get, the more materials break down, the worse the problem becomes, and the larger the magnetic field that is produced. The healthy home has the wiring checked periodically by a professional electrician for net current.

Plumbing

Clean, pure water is essential for good health (see pages 21 to 33 for more on water purification), but even clean water can become unhealthy and unsafe if your plumbing system isn't up to task.

Pipes

Leaks can saturate framing and surface coverings, leading to rot and mold infestation. Make a habit of inspecting the flexible hoses that supply your washing machine and dishwasher. These are notorious for bursting and can quickly soak and ruin a floor. Slow, insidious leaks can often be traced to the cheap plastic tube that supplies water to your refrigerator

Tip

Hire a professional to install and inspect your water heater.

Ideally, a storage tank heater should sit on a small concrete curb to raise it above ground.

Arc-Fault Circuit Interrupters

Replacing old wiring is expensive and may not be necessary as long as an inspection deems it to be in satisfactory condition. You can add an inexpensive line of defense to old circuits by replacing standard circuit breakers with arc-fault circuit interrupter (AFCI) breakers. Electrical code requires these breakers in new homes on all bedroom circuits, but they're also a good idea for bedroom circuits on old homes. When old wiring is damaged or decayed, ultimate failure often comes in the form of an electrical arc, which can easily cause a fire. AFCI breakers shut off the circuit at the first sign of an arc. AFCI breakers cost $25 to $35 and can be installed in minutes by an electrician.

icemaker. If you notice water near your refrigerator, don't assume it's condensation. In general, wherever you find unaccounted-for water, take the time to check nearby appliances and plumbing. Catching a small leak before it becomes a deluge could save you thousands of dollars and prevent a mold outbreak.

Faucets and hoses can also accidentally contaminate drinking water through a process called back-siphoning. Waste or other undrinkable water flows backward through one faucet and comes out when another faucet is opened. This can introduce deadly contaminates like bacteria or lawn chemicals into drinking water. Two common places where back-siphoning can occur is at the washing machine sink (when the drain backs up and the drain hose becomes submerged) and at outdoor faucets (someone leaves a garden hose in a puddle of water). You can prevent back-siphoning by installing a simple device called a vacuum breaker at each of these places. If you have an automated sprinkler system, make sure it is in working order and has back-siphoning protection.

Improperly installed waste and vent pipes can have a negative impact on air quality. Properly installed plumbing traps—the sharply curved pipes under every drain, generally called "P-traps"—protect against sewer gas contamination of your air. Sewer gas is a complex mixture of toxic and nontoxic gases, including hydrogen sulfide (which gives it a rotten egg smell) and ammonia. Nuisance-level concentrations can cause headaches and a general feeling of illness; at high concentrations, sewer gas

The Ground-Fault Circuit Interrupter

The ground-fault circuit interrupter, or GFCI, shuts off electrical current if a leak occurs. The National Electrical Code requires that all receptacles in potentially wet areas—such as bathrooms, garages, and yards—be protected by a GFCI against electrical shock.

A GFCI monitors how much electricity goes into an appliance and how much comes out. If there's a leak—a ground fault—and less electricity comes out than went in, the GFCI cuts the power within one-fortieth of a second—thrity times faster than a heartbeat! A GFCI can detect leakage levels far below those that would trip a circuit breaker or blow a fuse, and thus prevent fatal shock.

GFCIs can be installed in place of standard receptacles by anyone with electrical know-how. The built-in receptacle type is the most practical for residential use. GFCIs are required in new construction. They should be installed in all potentially wet areas (kitchens, laundries, bathrooms, workshops, and basements) of all older houses.

can be lethal. P-traps contain a small amount of water, which acts as a plug to prevent sewer gases from rising out through the drain. Traps are required by code, but in older houses, they may not be installed in basement floor drains or existing traps may be "S-traps," which are less effective than modern P-traps. If you smell a rotten-egg or sewage smell in the basement or near a sink, have a plumber check to see that a trap is present and properly installed.

The Water Heater

Hot water heaters can cause a host of safety problems. Does the hot water heater operate properly? Is the temperature setting too high? A setting of 120 degrees F is usually sufficient (140 degrees F if you have a dishwasher). Noise in hot water pipes when the hot water tap is turned on may indicate that the setting is too high.

A Healthy Home Has...

Heating System

- Solar gain heat with hot water in-floor radiant heat as backup.

- Ducts professionally cleaned before the start of each heating season.

- Furnace filters that are cleaned or changed regularly.

- Gas-fueled appliances checked annually for leaks, and each appliance with its own source of combustion air.

- A sound chimney with no cracks.

- Supply ducts to each room and a balanced level of return air throughout the house.

- Furnace and utilities enclosed in a soundproof room.

Cooling

- Natural methods of cooling rather than mechanical means.

- Clean, well-maintained mechanical air conditioning that is used only when necessary.

Electrical Systems

- Wiring that is adequate and up to date.

- Circuits listed at the service panel.

- GFCI-protected receptacles in the basement, kitchen, bathroom, and garage.

- Protective plates on all switches.

Plumbing

- Copper intake and supply pipes soldered with lead-free solder.

- A floor drain that has been checked for sewer gas entering the house.

- A pressure-relief valve installed on the hot water tank.

- Fixtures with individual shutoff valves and functioning traps.

SOUND

Bells, buzzers, and vacuum cleaners; mixers, coffee grinders, and garbage disposals; dogs barking, phones ringing, TVs blaring, doors slamming, kids arguing. Domestic cacophony can lead to thumping headaches and jangled nerves.

Noise is America's most widespread nuisance, outranking crime as the leading cause of neighborhood dissatisfaction. Even low levels of sound are annoying. It's an intrusion on our privacy and a strain on our nerves. It can be a source of great frustration, especially if nothing can be done about it.

Medical studies clearly identify noise as an important cause of physical and psychological stress, and stress has been linked with many of our common health problems—heart disease, high blood pressure, stroke, hypertension, hearing loss, headaches, fatigue, and hostility. And it's

worse for children. A 2001 study found that children living in noisy neighborhoods had higher blood pressure and heart rates, and they generally were more stressed out. A Swedish study found that people living near airports had higher blood pressure than those farther away.

The answer is not to tune out noise, but to learn how to cope with and quiet it. A good place to begin is in the home.

Creating an Oasis of Calm

Quieting a noisy house is not difficult. Start by analyzing the sources of noise. Wherever the offending noise is coming from, there's a good chance a simple home improvement will quiet it.

Exterior Noise

Most neighborhood noises enter the house through windows, doors, and exterior walls. Reduce this transmission by tightening up the places noise can seep through.

Windows

Windows and doors transmit a great deal of sound, and old single-pane windows with damaged glazing are almost as bad as having nothing at all. Adding panes of glass in the form of storm windows or doors on the noisy side of the house will reduce street noise by 50%. Replacing old single-pane windows with double-pane ones, and making a tight seal with weatherstripping and acoustic sealant will also reduce noise transmission.

Walls

As well as helping to retain heat, insulation creates mass that absorbs sound. If you're remodeling or adding on and noise is a concern, make sure all exterior walls are heavily insulated, regardless of climate. Insulation contractors can install insulation in finished walls without disturbing the wallboard or siding. After the insulation is in place, check the walls for air leaks. If you find any, stuff the area with insulation and seal the leak with acoustic sealant. You can also use the same interior-wall techniques listed on pages 120 to 121 to increase wall mass on exterior walls. Don't overlook exterior penetrations like outdoor faucets. Make sure they are tightly sealed.

Doors

Replace light or hollow-cored exterior doors with heavy, solid-cored doors. Make sure doors fit securely in their frames and that they are tightly sealed. All exterior doors and utility-room or basement doors should have sweeps installed on their bottom edges.

Draperies

Hanging heavy draperies won't help shut out exterior noise since noise intrusion from the outside is mostly in the low to middle frequencies. Draperies have few acoustic values in this range. They will, however, absorb sound coming from within the room.

Bushes, Berms, or Fences

To block unwanted traffic sounds from your house, plant thick hedges, bushes, and trees on the side toward the road. Viscous leaves also act as a filter, trapping some of the dust stirred up by passing vehicles.

If you have the space, earth berms help absorb sound between its source and the house. For further sound absorption, cover the mound with dense planting. A 6-foot earth berm topped with a dense hedge at least 4 feet high will reduce traffic noises.

If your house is downwind from a factory or schoolyard, the best remedy is to plant a windbreak between the house and the noise. A tight evergreen or deciduous hedge will provide protection as far downwind as twenty times its height. So a 9-foot-tall hedge can be planted as far as 180 feet from your house and still offer some protection.

Freestanding walls and tight fences covered with dense vines are also sound-absorbing. But hard surfaces are not. If noise really bothers you, avoid placing brick, flagstone, or concrete between your house and a source of noise.

How to Soundproof a Door

A properly soundproofed door can make an enormous difference in the amount of noise transmitted from the outside or between rooms. Consider soundproofing your basement or utility-room and garage doors if noise from a furnace or pump bothers you.

Cut acoustic ceiling tiles to fit over the whole door area. Cut a large notch in one tile to fit over the doorknob. Coat the backs of the tiles with a low-VOC adhesive (follow manufacturer's directions), and apply the tiles to the inside of the door.

Purchase an exterior door sweep long enough for your door. Cut the sweep to fit with a hacksaw. Secure the sweep to the bottom of the door with screws. The rubber part of the sweep should fit tightly against the threshold.

Add self-adhesive weatherstripping. Press weatherstripping into the joint between the doorstop and the jamb.

Interior Noise

First determine where the noise is coming from: within the room, outside the room, or within the **structure**. Once you've determined the source, find a way to reduce each noise to a tolerable level. Soundproofing a room may be as simple as sealing gaps around a door, or it may require rebuilding an entire wall or lowering a ceiling. You can muffle noise as it seeps into the room; contain it within a room so it doesn't leak out; mask the noise with additional, controlled noise; or prevent noise from entering a room.

Absorb Sound Within a Room

Soft, porous surfaces help absorb sound. Heavy draperies, wall-to-wall carpeting, large rugs, cork flooring, and upholstered furnishings each go a long way toward making a room quieter. Hard, slick surfaces—hardwood floors, plaster walls, glass windows—reflect sound and make a room noisy by bouncing sound around within it. A combination of hard and soft materials is the best solution acoustically.

Contain Noise Within a Room

To contain noise, add mass to the structure. Noise goes right through hollow doors, so replace them with solid-cored doors, especially in bedrooms, baths, kitchens, and playrooms. Less expensive, hollow-cored doors can be installed in quiet spots like closets and storage areas. Seal the bottoms of doors with sweep strips, and seal all cracks with weather-stripping.

Electrical receptacles placed back to back in a wall are another likely source of interior sound transmissions. Make sure all back-to-back wall receptacles are tightly installed. Add insulation around them if they're not. Ideally, receptacles and switches should be at least 3 feet apart.

If there is a gap between baseboard molding and the floor, sound can travel through that space. Seal these gaps with foam or low-VOC caulk.

Mask Noise

Mask noise with a constant, steady, controlled sound, such as a radio, fan, or white-noise maker. This final solution is a rather clumsy one since it adds to the background noise level.

Prevent Noise from Entering

If you can't find any air leaks, yet noise still bothers you, your best solution is to beef up wall mass, thus sacrificing some interior space. There are several ways to do this. The simplest is to line the noisy wall with bookshelves. Adding a layer of ⅝-inch fire-resistant drywall to the existing wall will also cut down on sound transmission. Attaching the additional drywall using resilient channels will make a further improvement. Resilient channels are simply strips of flexible metal that partially isolate the drywall from the surface beneath it.

If you're doing a major remodel and noise is a concern, ask your contractor about framing partition walls with a double row of staggered studs. This type of

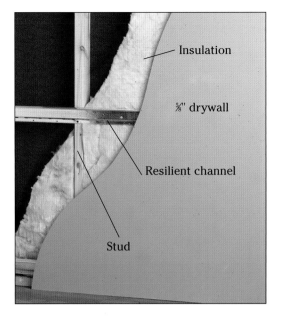

Insulation, ⅝-inch fire-resistant drywall, and resilient channel make for a wall that is significantly more resistant to sound transmission than standard construction, with only a small sacrifice of floor space.

construction allows surfaces on opposite sides of the partition to be attached to separate studs. When combined with insulation, ⅝-inch fire-resistant drywall, and resilient channel, a staggered-stud wall can have twice the sound-deadening effect of a standard wall.

Reducing Noise Within the Structure

The structure of a house can be a willing conduit for transmitting sound, but you can remedy noise seemingly built into the walls of a house.

Heating Ducts

If one heating duct is shared between two rooms, it provides an acoustic connection. Stop the noise of airflow by adding acoustic insulation inside the walls of the duct.

Water Pipes

Noisy water pipes are usually caused by air that has become trapped in the system by a fast-closing valve on a washing machine or other appliance—a phenomenon called "water hammer." These air

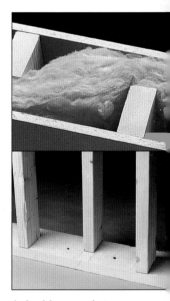

A double row of staggered wall studs helps isolate surfaces on either side of a common wall, lowering sound transmission between the rooms.

How to Seal Receptacles & Molding

If sound transmission between adjoining rooms is a problem, begin by making sure the common wall is adequately sealed. Outlet boxes can be a source of sound transmission, as can gaps between molding and the floor. Fortunately, there are simple solutions to these problems.

Remove the coverplate from the outlet. Take care not to touch any wires.

Place a sealing gasket over the outlet. Replace the coverplate.

Remove the base shoe molding. Use a pry bar to carefully remove the shoe. Place a scrap piece of wood between the bar and the baseboard to avoid marring the finish.

Spray low-VOC acoustical sealant into the gap between the floor and the baseboard. Reinstall the base shoe molding.

bubbles cause pipes to vibrate and bang against framing. The noise can resonate though your whole house, and the vibration can damage pipes and appliances

Where pipes are supported by walls, use an oversized pipe clamp and insert a gasket between the pipe and the clamp. Where pipes penetrate walls, the opening should be large enough to install a padding of insulation around the pipe. Finish the job by sealing off the padding at the face of the wall with acoustic sealant.

Eliminate air in the system by having a plumber install water hammer arresters near sources of noise. Do-it-yourself hammer arresters are available to install between the washing machine and the hose. Reduce water pressure by installing a pressure regulator in the water pipe and maintaining a water pressure of less than 45 pounds per square inch (psi).

Utility Rooms

Power-ventilated furnaces and water heaters are a good way to ensure no combustion byproducts seep into a structure, but they do have the drawback of noisy fans. If you hear it every time your water heater or furnace comes on, consider insulating your basement or utility room. Start with a heavy, solid-core door with a sweep on the bottom. Then, beef up walls and ceilings that adjoin living spaces.

Control Sound

Sound control is cumulative. The first steps you take will help a lot; subsequent steps will continue to help but with diminishing returns. Each of these tips contributes in its own way, and each is most effective in a given frequency range. You don't have to do them all. A modest amount of work can go a long way toward attaining a comfortable silence day in and day out.

A Healthy Home Has...

- Well-insulated walls and ceilings.
- Quiet appliances and ventilation fans.
- Solid-core doors with weatherstripping.
- A well-isolated attached garage

LIGHT

Interior lighting is an inexact science fraught with options and possibilities. When done well, it turns night into day, creates a positive mood, brightens household tasks, and increases security. When done poorly, it can increase fatigue, ruin mood, decrease performance, and cause headache and eyestrain.

Light has a powerful effect on the human body, influencing every aspect of being—mind, body, emotions, and spirit. Most endocrinologists contend light is the most important environmental input after food in controlling body function.

Natural Light

By far the healthiest form of light is natural sunlight. It uses no fuels and creates no pollution. And it's efficient: While energy emitted from an incandescent bulb is 90 percent heat and 10 percent light, energy from the sun is between 50 and 70

percent light. So it's important to use skylights and natural lighting through windows and glass doors whenever possible to allow the sun, rather than light bulbs, to light a healthy home.

But there are drawbacks to this free light. It's often accompanied by "hot spots" and heat. Natural light also changes throughout the day, so you're not going to get a constant light in either color or penetration. These seeming disadvantages can easily be turned into advantages.

Sunlight vs. Daylight

Sunlight and daylight are not the same. Sunlight is light direct from the sun that has not been scattered in the atmosphere. Because it contains infrared and ultraviolet light rays, sunlight can, without precautions, quickly cause overheating and rapid fading of fabrics.

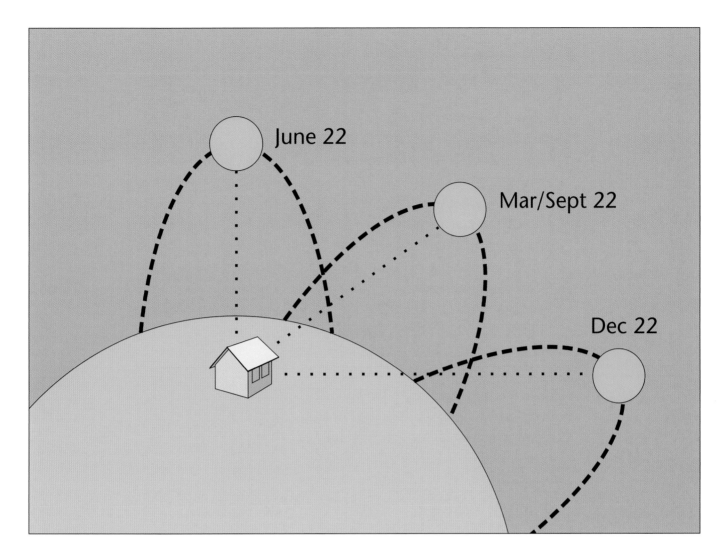

Daylight, which includes both light from the sun and light from the sky, is much less drastic in its effects. Daylight is largely diffuse and available for all windows, no matter what direction they face.

Natural light is transient, changing colors and directions as the sun makes its daily trek across the sky. The farther north you go, the more the seasons affect the journey of light, too. During the summer, for example, the sun rises in the northeast, arcs high in the sky, then sets almost northwest. It takes a different pathway in winter, when the sun stays much lower in the horizon. In winter, the sun rises south-southeast and quickly sets south-southwest.

Use this geometry to stay more in tune with the natural rhythms of the earth. Pay attention to what window light does in your house. Watch how it penetrates deeply into a room during certain seasons and at different times of day. Experience its playfulness as well as its generosity. Analyze its color and character so you'll know how to use it.

Types of Light

Bluish and diffuse, cool north light is mostly indirect light reflected from the sky. Artists prefer it for its uniform, shadowless character.

More than light from any other direction, south light provides heat as well as illumination. It's bright and direct, casting

To make the most of the sunlight available to your home, be aware of the seasonal path of the sun and how its light enters windows and skylights at different times of the year.

sharp interior shadows and maybe even causing glare. South light is great for family gathering places and passive-solar spaces.

East-facing rooms have direct light in the morning. Such light is cool in hue because much of its red wavelengths are absorbed into the moist morning atmosphere. East-facing windows are best for your kitchen and breakfast room, and your bedroom if you're an early riser.

West-facing rooms receive direct light in late afternoon, which can be quite intense in both brightness and heat. Evening light has a warm pink, reddish, or orange hue. Living rooms benefit from having a west-facing window, creating a relaxing atmosphere for winding down after a hard day. Be sure all west-facing windows have good, workable shades; otherwise, sunlight can cause overheating.

Sunlight Problems

In the name of energy efficiency, today's windows come with a parade of glass treatments, each one proclaimed the best for a specific function. The only thing wrong with them is the spectrum of light they admit. The healthiest light contains the full spectrum of the sun. While ordinary window glass admits a fuller spectrum of visible light, ultraviolet light is blocked more at certain ranges of the spectrum than at others. For example, clear window glass transmits from 67 to 79 percent across the spectrum of UV light; low-E window glass admits from 51 to 63 percent of UV light.

When choosing your windows, base your decision on color, visible light, and ultraviolet light, as well as which ones will work best with your heating and cooling system. Certain glazing will save you costs and possibly increase your comfort level. If you choose a high-performance glazing window versus clear glass, you may sacrifice a little visible light but, from an energy-consumption standpoint, you'll use less energy for the rest of your house. An optimal choice would be to specify different glazing choices on each elevation of your house to achieve the best results.

There's lots of latitude for getting the right light you need. But there are a few problems to conquer, including fading, glare, and overheating.

Fading

Because sunlight contains infrared and ultraviolet light rays in addition to visible light, it causes deterioration of fabrics in carpets, upholstery, and draperies, as well as aging and bleaching of wood, plastics, photographs and paintings. Wet fabric fades more quickly than dry. Likewise, certain pigments are more apt to fade than others. Paint finishes, especially glossy ones, are not as susceptible as fabrics. Fiberglass, polyester, and acrylic are more resistant to fading than nylon, acetate, or rayon. Natural fibers—cotton, jute, sisal, wool, and silk—have poor resistance to sunlight damage. A fabric is more fade-resistant when the fiber is thick, the weave is tight, the finish is shiny or bright, and the color is highly reflective. For all surfaces, the degree of fading is regulated by the kind and intensity of light and by the time of exposure.

The trick is to find a happy medium between exposure and protection. In rooms receiving a lot of sunlight, rotate or move carpets, upholstery, fabrics of all kinds, woods, and other objects from time to time so all areas receive equal expo-

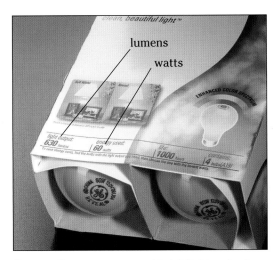

lumens

watts

"Lumens" are a measure of total light output. "Watts" are a measure of energy consumption. To get the brightest, most efficient bulb, look for the most lumens per watt.

shadow, perhaps—that makes a house special.

A Word About Bulbs

When buying light bulbs, pay attention to lumen rating, not wattage. Lumens measure the total light output. The brightest bulb—the one that produces the most lumens—may or may not have the most wattage.

One of the first decisions you have to make is what type of light bulb to use. As far as how they work, you have two options: incandescent or fluorescent. Both types create light by running electrical current through some sort of medium that glows when energized.

The incandescent bulb has a tungsten filament that glows as electrical current passes through it. Fluorescent bulbs are mercury-vapor-filled chambers coated with phosphors that glow when current flowing through the vapor causes an ultraviolet arc. Halogen lights are a relatively new type of incandescent bulb. Compact fluorescents, as the name implies, are a newer type of fluorescent bulb.

For indoor lighting, the marketplace offers the following options.

Standard Incandescent Bulb

This hasn't changed much since Thomas Edison invented the lightbulb more than a century ago. It provides a steady, pleasant, warm light similar to that of the sun. For these reasons, it is the most preferred bulb for the home. Good for both task and background lighting, it produces the most flattering light and a warmer emotional resonance, perhaps because it's similar to candlelight and firelight. Because incandescent bulbs produce a lot of heat, they are not energy efficient. Inexpensive to buy but costly to use, they don't last as long as other types of bulbs, and they dim with age.

Fluorescent Tube

This costs more to buy but is inexpensive to use because it wastes less energy giving off heat, and lasts longer than incandescents (halogens included). Fluorescents produce a diffuse, bright white, cool light without harsh shadows and hot spots. Newer types of fluorescents don't have the color distortion common in older types. Those operated on magnetic ballasts produce a subtle flicker or hum (which contributes to headache, eyestrain, and general annoyance), so it's best to choose fluorescents with electronic ballasts.

Compact Flourescent

Relatively new to the marketplace, this small fluorescent-type bulb is highly energy efficient, cheap to use, and long-lasting. Though expensive to buy, it pays for itself in efficiency. Most have a screw base that fits into regular incandescent sockets, sometimes with the aid of an adapter. Their light is much closer to the quality of incandescent light, and they provide very good color rendition. In choosing a compact fluorescent bulb, first figure out which wattage of incandescent bulb would provide the brightness you desire, then divide that by three. So, if you want something comparable to a 75-watt incandescent, you'd choose a 26-watt compact fluorescent.

Halogen

A relatively new invention, used a lot in modern design, the small halogen bulb emits a brilliant, crisp, white light that's cooler than incandescents, making it a favorite choice for task and spot lighting. Halogens last much longer than incandescents and dim little with age. Disadvantages are the intense heat they give out, the fact that they require special light sockets, and their fragility. They require special handling. Never touch the bulb with your bare fingers as they are highly sensitive to skin oils. Wear cotton gloves or handle them with tissues.

Full Spectrum

Manufacturers of both fluorescent and incandescent bulbs make full-spectrum bulbs designed to simulate the full spectrum of sunlight while providing a bright, efficient, diffuse light. Though the color of the light is true, none of them exactly

Safety Tips

- Match bulb wattage to fixture rating.
- Keep incandescent or halogen bulbs away from flammable materials such as draperies.
- Retrofit older halogen lamps with a glass filter that both reduces shattering risks and filters out ultraviolet radiation.
- Do not use halogen floor lamps in children's rooms.
- Install a wire guard on older torchieres to keep the bulb from coming in contact with fabric.
- Never use a halogen bulb that is cracked or broken; it could shatter and cause injury or property damage.
- Use a halogen bulb with a bulb under 300 watts, even in lamps rated for up to 500 watts. These bulbs get exceedingly hot—up to 650 degrees F.
- Keep bulbs away from splashing water, which might cause the bulb to break.
- Always illuminate stairs. Three-way switches are essential, with one at the top and one at the bottom of the stairway.

mimics sunlight. Some manufacturers tout health benefits of full-spectrum bulbs, specifically that they help minimize seasonal affective disorder, or SAD, a type of winter-time depression caused by biochemical imbalance in the body. Full-spectrum bulbs do reduce eyestrain, but studies show that SAD is corrected more with intensity of light than with color spectrum. Regular, prolonged exposure to light at sunlight-like intensities (many hundreds of times greater than normal artificial levels) during periods of SAD-related depression can have a significant effect on symptoms.

A major drawback of full-spectrum bulbs is the lack of consistency among manufacturers; some full-spectrum bulbs contain ultraviolet rays, while others do not. Be sure to read the label so you know what you are buying.

A Healthy Home Has...

- A good mix of natural and artificial lighting.

- Windows on two sides of each room.

- Window area equaling at least one-tenth of the room's floor area.

- Shading on south-facing windows and skylights.

- Overall background lighting in each room with a switch right inside the door.

- Bulbs that produce light resembling the spectrum of daylight.

- Task lighting at the sink, stovetop, and countertop in the kitchen.

- Desks, tables, and computers placed at right angles to windows.

SAFETY

Your home may be your castle, but it's also where you're most likely to have an accident. According to the National Safety Council, in American homes there is a disabling injury every four seconds, and a fatal injury every sixteen minutes.

Retrofitting your house for safety is mostly a matter of common sense and little cash outlay. It's all those things you've probably already thought about but perhaps haven't gotten around to doing—smoke detectors, outdoor lighting, nonskid mats under carpets and rugs, bathmats near the tub, secure stair railings, and lockable storage space for medicines and other dangerous substances.

Falls & Accidents

Falls are the number-one form of accident in the home. They can be severely disabling, even fatal. Falls took the lives of 8,000 U.S. citizens in 2002, four out of five of them over the age of 65. Loose scatter rugs, slippery floors, dimmed lights, electrical cords stretched across corridors, and objects left on stairs are common culprits.

You must first find hazards before you can eliminate them. Take a walk through your house periodically and assess it for trip-and-fall hazards. Check floors for slippery areas. Look for obstacles that can make you trip. Be aware of hazards that can appear unexpectedly. The National Safety Council advises specific awareness when it comes to the following conditions or areas.

Slippery Floors

Don't wax floors to a slippery luster—safety is vastly more important than aesthetics. Scatter rugs can slide, taking you with them. If a rug doesn't have a nonskid backing, place a nonslip rug mat under the rug. Never use a rug at the top or bottom of a stairway. A carpet or rug that doesn't lie flat can catch your foot and make you stumble. Smooth out wrinkles and folds, and tack down loose edges. Repair frayed edges and rips. When buying a new rug or carpet, pass up those long, thick piles. They won't give you firm footing. Instead, choose a short, dense pile and install it over a good-quality, medium-thick pad.

Crowded Traffic Lanes

Keep traffic lanes free and clear. People should be able to walk through rooms without detouring around furniture. People should be able to move through doorways and halls without squeezing past obstacles.

Areas between bedrooms and bathrooms should always be clear. Don't pile items on stairs or use stairs as storage areas.

Outdoor Conditions

Check your yard and other outdoor areas for hazards. Patch broken walks and driveways, and fill in lawn and garden holes. Put away garden tools and hoses, and get rid of rocks, loose boards, and other obstacles that can make people stumble. Clear wet leaves and snow from walkways, steps, and porches; and sprinkle icy patches with salt. Provide doormats at entrances so people can wipe snow and mud from their shoes and not track it onto your floors.

Poor Lighting

Darkness can turn any room into an obstacle course. Shadows can hide hazards. Reduce the risk of injury with plenty of good, strong light. Install light switches near doorways so you never need to walk through a dark room to turn on a light. A lamp that's easily reached from your bed will help you avoid nighttime falls. Nightlights in the bathroom and hall add to your safety. Light all steps well, including the first and last steps, where most falls happen.

Protect Vulnerable Members of the Household

If you have toddlers in the house, or if they visit, protect them from places where they could fall and get hurt. Install safety gates at the tops and bottoms of stairs and make sure balcony areas are safe and guard rails can't be climbed.

Elderly people are most vulnerable to falls. Make sure all stairs have sturdy railings. Make sure all rooms have adequate overall lighting. Place night-lights on the route from bedroom to bathroom.

Bathrooms are especially hazardous when it comes to falls, especially for the elderly. Make sure the toilet and tub areas have grab bars and towel racks that are anchored to the framing. It's also a good idea to install a phone in the bathroom in case an elderly member of the household falls (see page 142).

Poisons

About 90 percent of accidental poisonings occur in the home, and the typical victim is a child under the age of six. More children die of poisoning each year than of all infectious diseases combined.

Cleaning substances, plants, and medicines are the most commonly identified culprits, but pesticides pose a real health hazard, too. They are the second most frequent cause of poisoning in young children, following medicines.

What can you do to make your home safe from poisonings? Prevention is the best cure. Go through all cabinets and drawers in your house periodically and weed out toxic substances. These include disinfectants, ammonia, insecticides, bleach, mothballs, kerosene, paint thinner, prescription drugs, cosmetics, detergents, drain and oven cleaners, nail polish and nail polish remover, rubbing alcohol, perfumes, hydrogen peroxide, and all acids. Dispose of those you no longer need in an ecologically safe manner (see pages 71 to 76). Analyze the toxicity of those you keep. Store highly toxic substances under lock and key in a cool, dry place where children and pets cannot find them.

Keep the telephone number of your local poison control center posted near each telephone, and don't hesitate to use it.

Slippery rugs are an easy-to-fix falling hazard. Purchase nonslip rug mats to go under rugs that have smooth backs. They're available at hardware and carpet stores.

Toilets present a drowning hazard for toddlers. Toilet latches keep toddlers from lifting the lid. Latches can quickly and easily be installed without making any permanent modification to the toilet.

Make a list of essential emergency numbers, including poison control, police and fire, and doctors, and place it by the most-often-used phone in the house.

If you think you or another family member has ingested a poisonous substance, call. Have the container of the substance with you when you call so you can help emergency personnel give you the proper guidance. The person answering the phone will be able to tell you whether there is a hazard, what action to take next, and, if necessary, the person will relay information to a hospital and/or emergency personnel.

Keep the phone numbers of your doctor, medical emergency clinics, and other emergency numbers near your telephone, too, and be sure your babysitter knows where these numbers are posted.

Fire

Although hotel fires receive the most notoriety, the majority of fire deaths and injuries occur at home. Every year in the U.S., approximately 5,000 people are killed and more than 40,000 are injured by fires at home. In addition, more than $8 billion worth of property is damaged by home fires. Many fire victims die from inhalation of smoke and toxic gases, not burns. Most deaths and injuries occur in fires that happen at night while victims are asleep.

To be safe, do two things: Exercise fire prevention, and make a plan so that everyone in the house knows what to do if a fire occurs.

The first rule of fire prevention is caution—don't start the fire that kills you. It's a bit simplistic but nevertheless important. Beware of hazardous situations and remedy them immediately.

Prevent Kitchen Fires

To prevent kitchen fires, the simplest suggestion is to keep your kitchen clean.

Grease will burst into flame when heated to its ignition point, so clean the areas where grease collects—the vent hood, the broiler, and any drain pans.

Use pot holders and turn pot handles away from the front of the range so they won't be dropped or knocked over. Don't leave food cooking while you become engrossed in a TV show or a phone conversation. If you must answer the telephone in another room, carry a spoon or potholder with you as a reminder you left something cooking. Use a timer. Check for combustible materials, like curtains or a paper-covered shelf, near the burners.

Never use towels or clothing instead of potholders. Exercise care with clothing while cooking. Fires caused by dangling sleeves, scarves, and ties are common. If you have long hair, tie it back while cooking. When cooking on a gas stove, never put small pots and pans on large burners and never let the flame rise up the sides of the pot.

Unplug countertop appliances when not in use. Make sure the stove is off when not in use. Do not use flammable aerosols in the kitchen.

Appliance & Cord Safety

Major appliances all over the house present fire hazards. Televisions, stereos, microwaves, computers, and other electronic equipment generate a lot of heat, so they need air around them. Don't place them tightly in a bookcase or flat against a wall.

Always turn off the appliance before unplugging it. If you need to work on an appliance for any reason, unplug it first. Be especially cautious with toasters. If you need to remove something that's stuck inside, unplug the toaster first. When you

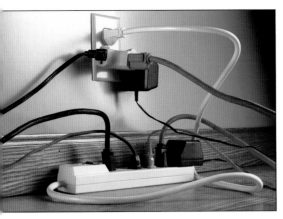

Look familiar? If you have outlets that are sprouting multiple power strips and extension cords, it's a signal that a call to an electrician is in order. Have an electrician add additional receptacles or circuits.

unplug an appliance, grasp the plug, not the cord.

Clothes dryers can be fire hazards if they aren't properly maintained. Always clean out the lint trap before starting a new load. If you have an electric dryer, get in the habit of cleaning out the flexible pipe that runs to the vent. If you have a gas dryer, ask the technician to clean out the dryer vent whenever you have your heating system inspected. Moving a gas dryer yourself can rupture the gas line and cause a leak. Let a professional take care of it instead.

Extension cords and surge strips are common sources of electrical fires. Do not put furniture on top of a cord or run cords underneath carpets or rugs. Never nail down or staple a cord; use tape, instead. Never place a cord near anything hot or drape it over a hot surface, such as a radiator. Outdoors, use only cords marked for outdoor use. Be careful not to overload electrical outlets, extension cords, and power strips.

Other Fire Hazards

In addition to safety checks on heating systems and major appliances, some common household products are potential fire hazards:

Aerosols

Aerosols contain gases that expand when heated, creating pressure that may make the can explode. In addition, aerosols may contain chemicals that produce harmful fumes when heated. The propellant used in some aerosols is extremely flammable. Spraying some hair sprays, for example, produces a mist of liquid and gas, both flammable. If done near a heat source, such as a hair dryer or kitchen range, the result could be disastrous. The best advice is to avoid aerosols altogether.

Gasoline-Powered Equipment

Lawn mowers, chain saws, and other gasoline-powered equipment present fire hazards both in their use and in gasoline storage. Never refuel this equipment while it is running, or even while the engine is off but still hot. Gasoline spilled onto a hot engine will instantly vaporize and can burst into flame, which can in turn run up to the gas can you're holding and explode in flames. Even when done properly, fueling and refueling should be done outdoors rather than in the garage or storage shed. Store gasoline in its original

Unplug your electric dryer and move it away from the wall. Remove the vent pipe by loosening the clamp that holds it in place. Remove any lint that has built up in the pipe. Use a vacuum cleaner hose, if necessary.

Extinguishing Common Kitchen Fires

If oil catches fire in a pan on the stove, do not move the pan or try to carry the pan outside. Moving the pan may spread the fire, fan the flames, or burn you. Instead, follow these steps:

- Put a lid over the pan to cut off air.
- Turn off the burner if it is safe to do so.
- Do not touch the pan for 30 minutes.
- Never use water or an ordinary fire extinguisher to put out an oil or grease fire.

In the event of an oven or broiler fire:

- Close the oven or broiler door
- Turn off the oven.

container away from the house, preferably in a detached garage. Store lawnmowers outside the home and outside any structure attached to the house.

Volatile Substances

Keep volatile chemicals, such as fertilizers, turpentine, kerosene, and gasoline, in their original containers and in a locked storage area away from the house. Both kerosene and gasoline can leak fumes when stored. If the room in which they are stored is not properly ventilated, fumes can grow so dense that they can easily catch fire if a spark is generated.

Oily Rags

When you clean up after painting or any other project that involves flammable liquids, be as careful with your cleaning tools as you are with the flammable liquids themselves. If rags soaked with turpentine, paint thinner, lacquer, or oil-based paint are left in a pile, fumes can build up and combust with only the slightest spark. It's best to put oily and greasy rags in a metal can filled with sand, put the can outside, away from the house, then throw it out with the trash.

Holiday Decorations

Electrical fires and other burning accidents have ruined many a Christmas. If you buy a live tree each year, make sure it's fresh (green, with no dropping needles, and a trunk sticky with sap) and keep it in a sturdy stand away from all heat sources. Cut off a couple of inches at the bottom so the trunk can take in water, and keep the tree well watered at all times. Don't leave tree lights on when the tree is unattended, and don't leave small children unattended around Christmas trees. If you buy an artificial tree, choose one tested and labeled as fire resistant. Keep a fire extinguisher near the exit of the room where you've placed the tree and make sure there is a smoke detector nearby. Once the tree is dried out, dispose of it. Don't leave it on the porch or anywhere near the house. And don't burn it in the fireplace!

Candles

Never leave a lit candle unattended. Extinguish all candles before leaving a room or going to sleep. Be sure candles aren't placed near anything flammable, including Christmas trees and wreaths. Be cautious of curtains, drapes, scarves, and loose clothing that can billow in a breeze and touch the candle flame. Make sure candles are secure in their holders and placed where they will not be knocked down or blown over. Never leave children alone in a room with lit candles. If you have young children or pets at home, place lit candles out of their reach. Do not permit children to keep or use candles or incense in their rooms.

Lightning

A house standing alone is a prime target for a lightning strike. If you have lots of electrical storms in your area and your house is located on a high, exposed site, you may want to install a lightning rod on the roof. A lightning rod will intercept electrical charges before they strike a building and will divert them to the ground. A lightning rod won't protect you from injury caused by lightning striking a telephone wire while you're talking on the phone. This is not uncommon. Don't have telephones installed near wet areas, electrical appliances, and other fixtures that are conductive to the ground.

Fire Safety

A house fire can be a killer in less than three minutes. Safe practices at home are part of a family's fire protection plan. It's critical that all family members be prepared to react quickly should a fire occur.

Fire Escape Plan

Don't plan to make a plan—do it now! Identify two exits out of every room and establish a meeting place outside, probably a neighbor's house, where you can call 911. Ensure that family members with special needs (such as someone who is ill or frail, or small children) have a buddy to help them get out safely.

As you discuss the plan with young children, don't overload them. Concentrate on escape routes from their bedrooms. Place either chain or rope ladders near upstairs windows. The best ladders are those with spacers holding the ladder away from the house.

Practice makes perfect. Hold both scheduled and unscheduled drills with your family. Drill and drill again. Once you've mastered the escape process, hold a drill when family members are sleeping so you can test everyone's ability to wake up and respond to the smoke alarm. If someone doesn't awaken on his or her own, assign a buddy to help them waken and escape. Have everyone learn the following escape tips.

- **Feel a door before you open it.** Feel it at the top and on the knob. If it's hot, don't open it—look for a secondary route.
- **Crawl on your hands and knees.** This keeps your head at just the right height—below most of the rising smoke and heat and above the dense toxic gases that settle near the floor.
- **Keep a damp cloth over your nose and mouth, if possible.** This filters out most of the deadly smoke. Remember, over 80 percent of fire deaths are from smoke inhalation.
- **Don't run.** Running fans the flames. If your clothing does catch fire, roll over to smother the flames.
- **Don't delay in escaping.** Don't take time to save your favorite teddy bear, your great-grandmother's clock, your stamp collection, or even your pet dog or cat. This same principle applies after you're out—don't re-enter for anything!
- **Stop, Drop, Roll.** Teach every family member to "Stop, drop, and roll" if clothes catch fire.

Smoke Detectors

When properly installed and maintained, the smoke detector is one of the best and least expensive ways to provide early warning when a fire begins. An alarm sounds before the concentration of smoke reaches a dangerous level, or before the fire becomes too intense. The risk of dying from fire is twice as high in homes that do not have functioning detectors. If you don't have smoke detectors in your house, get them now! There are two basic types to choose from.

Ionization detectors: Though these used to be the recommended type (and the cheapest at around $6 for a battery-powered unit), they haven't lived up to their advertising and are not the best type when it comes to detecting fires. In addition, they contain a small amount of radioactive material (Americium 241, a waste product from nuclear reactors) sandwiched between thin layers of gold and silver foil, which makes them a hazard. If tampered with, crushed in disposal, or incinerated, this radioactive material may be ingested or inhaled. It is easily absorbed into the body from the lungs or intestines and causes cancer and genetic injury, in addition to other negative health effects. Since Americium 241 has a half-life of 458 years, ionization smoke detectors will inevitably be a greater hazard to future generations rather than our own since it is encapsulated on a ceiling or wall fixture for our short period of use. If you have an ionizing smoke detector, it should be classified as hazardous waste and returned to the manufacturer for disposal.

Photoelectric detectors: Though more expensive (costing around $32 for a stand-alone device), photoelectric smoke detectors are more sensitive to smoke than the ionizing type and are now considered to be superior at detecting both a flaming fire and a smoldering one. According to tests performed by the U.S. National Bureau of Standards, improved photoelectric detectors provide two to three times more chance of escape than the ionizing type does. Photoelectric detectors use a tiny beam of light to detect smoke particles, activating the photoelectric cell, and setting off an alarm. What's more, photoelectric detectors are less sensitive to humidity and cooking smoke, which means fewer false alarms.

Smoke detectors also differ by power source. Batteries in battery-powered

How to Replace a Smoke Detector

If the smoke detectors in your house are more than ten years old, replace them with new photoelectric detectors. If you have hardwired units, make sure you replace all the detectors with the same brand.

Turn off the power to the smoke detectors at the service panel. Remove the first smoke detector by twisting it off its base. Double check that the power is off with a circuit tester. Then, disconnect the circuit wires from the detector by unscrewing the wire nuts. Unscrew the base from the ceiling.

Thread the circuit wires through the new base and attach the base to the ceiling. Connect the black lead wire from the detector to the black circuit wires and the white lead wire to the white circuit wires. Connect the odd-colored lead (shown red here) to the red wires. Twist the detector into its base. Repeat for all the other detectors smoke detectors last approximately one year. When the battery begins to lose power and needs to be replaced, the detector emits "beeps" every minute or so, sometimes for a week or longer. Detectors operating on household current have backup batteries so they operate during power failures. Plug-in units must be located near an electric outlet where they will not be unplugged or turned off by a wall switch. Never use an extension cord with a plug-in unit.

Heat detectors are also available, sometimes as part of a smoke detector, sometimes as a separate unit costing between $10 and $20. These sense the heat from a fire to trigger an alarm or sprinkler system, but they do not detect smoke. Heat detectors add protection, but are not effective early warning devices by themselves. Because they must be very close to a fire to be set off, they're useful in places where smoke detectors can be fooled, such as a kitchen. They're also useful in areas where smoke detectors cannot function because it is too hot or too cold. Sometimes they're combined with home break-in alarm equipment to provide a total home security system connected to your local fire and police services.

Because smoke rises, the best location for smoke detectors is on the ceiling or high on an inside wall just below the ceiling. Install at least one on each level of the house, always having one between sleeping areas and the rest of the house. As a general guideline, on the first floor the detector should be placed on the ceiling at the base of the staircase or in the living room. For basements, at the bottom of the stairway is best. In the kitchen and bath, choose a location away from the path of steam and cooking vapors, which can result in false alarms. Don't install smoke detectors near windows, doors, or ducts where drafts might interfere with their operation.

Research shows 10 to 15 percent of smoke alarms in houses do not work properly, so it's important to change the battery regularly and check monthly that smoke alarms are working. Fire officials recommend that you change your batteries at the same time each year, say on July 4th or at the same time you turn your clock back each year for the end of Daylight Savings time. Smoke detectors should be replaced at least once every ten years.

Fire Extinguishers

If fire breaks out, you're going to have to quickly decide whether to fight it or flee. If you decide to fight, always keep your back to the door so you can escape if the fire begins to spread.

Deciding whether a fire is extinguishable or not can be a tough call. As a general guideline, a fire started by an electrical appliance would be difficult to extinguish. The same is true with a wall fire due to electrical wiring. These kinds of fires often smolder deep within the wiring and

Fire-Retardant Latex Paint

Fire-retardant latex paints are available for interior ceilings, walls, and trim. When attacked by flame, the coating on these paints chars, foams, and expands to form a thick cellular blanket that reduces heat penetration, thus retarding flame spread and minimizing smoke. It's ideal for a workshop or utility room.

Keep a fire extinguisher in the kitchen and make sure everyone knows how to use it. Make sure the fire extinguisher carries the Underwriters Laboratories seal and is ABC rated (inset).

are difficult to get to. On the other hand, you'll probably be able to put out a grease fire in a skillet or a fire in a trash can. Throw baking soda (not water) onto a grease fire, or cover it with a lid, and turn off the flame. A trash-can fire can also be put out with a lid of some kind. Any flat object, like a cookie sheet or a large pan, will smother the fire by cutting off its oxygen. If you have any doubt about your ability to put out the fire, close the door on it, warn others, and go elsewhere to call the fire department.

The best method of extinguishing a house fire is by using a fire extinguisher. A multipurpose extinguisher—marked "ABC"—is recommended for the home. This extinguisher is filled with a dry chemical that interrupts the chemical chain reaction of fire and, with ordinary combustibles, smothers the fire. It won't completely extinguish a deep upholstery

fire, however. Further action is needed, such as smothering it outside the house. Avoid purchasing fire extinguishers that use a halon propellant, which contributes to ozone-layer depletion. Consult with a salesperson from a local safety equipment store, fire extinguisher store, or hardware store to determine which extinguisher meets your needs. Then learn how to use and maintain it.

The location of fire extinguishers is critical because, when a fire erupts, you won't have time to go looking for one. Every house is different, but here are a few general guidelines:

- Keep an extinguisher near an outside door, not in a dead-end corner where you could be trapped.
- Hang the kitchen extinguisher so you don't have to reach across stove-top flames to get it.
- Place extinguishers in bedrooms, garages, and workshop areas.

If you've already got extinguishers, check to make sure they're ABC-type models. Also be sure they haven't passed their expiration dates and that they have been recently inspected.

Sprinkler Systems

Combined with smoke alarms, automatic sprinkler systems cut the risk of dying in a home fire by 82 percent compared to having neither. If you are renovating or planning to build a new home, consider

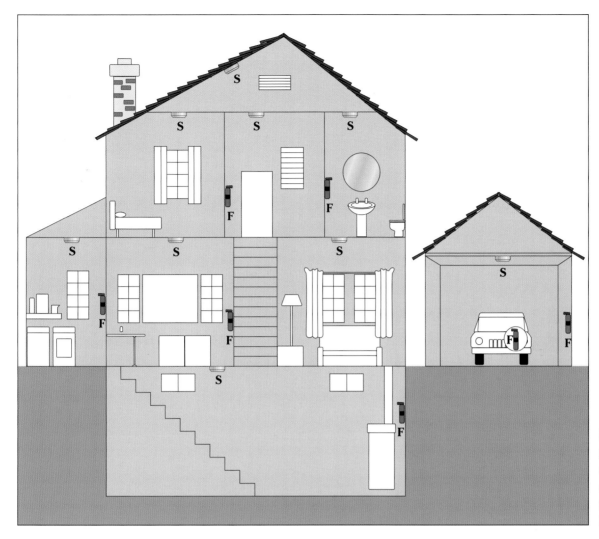

Place fire extinguishers (F) and smoke detectors (S) throughout the house.

having a fire sprinkler system installed. Cost is an additional 1 to 1.5 percent of overall cost of new construction, according to the Home Safety Council. Cost is higher in a renovation project. You may be able to get a discount on your insurance, depending on the type of coverage you have. Discounts range between 5 to 15 percent.

Residential sprinkler systems work the same way sprinkler systems in hotels do, only much more efficiently and generally a lot less conspicuously. A network of piping installed behind the walls and ceilings holds sprinklers at various junctures. They're specially designed to react only to the high temperature of a fire. When they activate, they douse the flames below with water. Usually only one sprinkler, the one closest to the fire, will open. At a minimum, one sprinkler will cover a 12 × 12-foot area. Usually, only one sprinkler is needed for a 20 × 20-foot bedroom.

Because they react when the fire is small, sprinklers dramatically limit fire and smoke. As a result of this quick response, far less water is put on the fire, typically only 25 gallons per minute. The sprinkler's quick response slows a fire's dangerous growth and spread, giving you and your family the time you need to safely escape and call the fire department.

How to Install a Fire Escape Ladder

Adding fire escape ladders to second floor windows is a good idea. Most inexpensive models don't attach permanently to the window, though, and it's all too easy for them to get stuffed in a closet. Look for models that can be built into a cabinet below the window, like the model shown below (see page 171 for more information).

Use a stud finder to locate two studs below a second-story window sill. There should be 14 ½" between the edges of the pair of studs. Mark a horizontal line from stud edge to stud edge 4" below the sill. Mark another horizontal line 17" below the top line. Mark the edges of the studs between the two lines (you should have a 14 ½" × 17" rectangle).

Use a stud finder with live-wire detector or make a small hole in the center of the rectangle, and make sure there is no wiring in the wall. Cut out the rectangle with a drywall saw.

Place the fire escape cabinet in the opening. Drill pilot holes for the mounting screws (follow manufacturer's instructions). Drive the mounting screws. Fold the ladder into the cabinet as directed by the manufacturer.

How to Install a Bathroom Phone Without Running New Wires

A phone in the bathroom can be a lifeline if an elderly or disabled member of the household has a fall. Fortunately, you don't have to run new telephone wires or install jacks to add a phone in your bathroom. All you need is an electrical receptacle and phone-line-to-receptacle adapter kit. The system installs in minutes. Make sure you use a corded phone with buttons on the handset so a fallen person can pull the handset to him- or herself from the floor.

Plug the telephone wire from an existing telephone jack into either jack on the side of the transmitter unit. (It's important to plug in the transmitter before the receiver . In the event of a problem, unplug both and start again.)

Plug the base unit transmitter into a 120-volt receptacle. To use a phone at the existing jack location, plug that phone into the extra jack on the side of the base unit transmitter.

Plug the wireless phone-jack receiver module into a 120-volt receptacle in the bathroom near the tub or toilet. Plug a telephone into the jack on the receiver unit. There should now be a dial tone on the added phone line.

A Healthy Home Has...

KITCHEN

- A sturdy step stool to reach uppermost shelves.
- Knives stored out of reach of children.
- Knives kept in a knife block or secure rack—not loose in drawers.
- Exhaust fans vented to the outside.
- Exhaust fan filters cleaned regularly.
- Flammable objects, such as dishtowels and curtains, at least three feet away from the cooktop.
- Combustible materials (recipe cards, potholders, matches, etc.) not kept on the stove top.
- Baking soda near the stove for grease fires.
- A fire extinguisher, rated ABC.
- Cleaning products and toxic substances stored under lock and key in a cool, dry place.

BATHROOM

- Ground-fault circuit interrupter (GFCI) on every outlet.
- Floors and tubs with nonslip, textured surfaces.
- Countertops and shower doors with rounded edges.
- Medicine cabinets with no dangerous drugs or toxic chemicals.
- Hot-water temperature no higher than 130 degrees F.

LIVING AREA

- Room to move around without tripping over objects or furniture.
- A metal screen across the mouth of a fireplace.

BEDROOM

- Clear paths from the doors to the beds.
- Overall general room lighting, with switches right inside the doors.
- Well-lit closets.
- Closet shelves that are neat and organized.

STAIRS & HALLWAYS

- Three-way switches, with one at the top and one at the bottom of the stairs and at either end of a long hallway.
- Firmly attached carpeting.
- Sturdy handrails.

WORKSHOP

- GFCI-protected receptacles.
- A clean, unobstructed floor.
- Instructions for all power tools on file.
- Blades of tools protected with blade guards.
- Safely stored glues, paints, and cleaners.
- Minimal use of extension cords.

GARAGE

- An automatic garage door with an operable reverse.
- Well-organized storage areas.
- Flammable products stored in an approved storage locker.

YARD

- Children's slides, swings, and other outdoor play equipment inspected annually for rusty chains, bent or loose bars, and general stability.
- Walks and driveways in good repair.
- A yard free of litter—especially nails, broken glass, tin cans, splintered wood, and other dangers.
- All outdoor circuits protected by a GFCI.
- Nonslip decks and patios.
- Grills at least three feet away from other objects, including the house and shrubs or bushes.

SECURITY

Locking your doors and windows is a fact of life in twenty-first-century America. In 2002, according to the FBI, there were 2.1 million robberies nationwide; property crime loss topped a whopping $16.6 billion. That's not even the whole story. According to the National Crime Victimization Survey, only 40 percent of property-related crimes are reported.

Having a house that's unattractive to burglars is not just a matter of luck. And you don't need an expensive security system. Common sense and beefing up physical security go a long way toward protecting your family against the threat of home invasion, burglary, and forced entry.

Deterrence

The best possible security is a house and yard that isn't an attractive target for criminals. Take a few simple steps, and burglars won't even want to get near your home.

Light

Burglars don't like to be in the spotlight, whether it's trained on the porch, in the yard, or at any of the entrances to house or garage. But you don't want your property to look like the aurora borealis at night, either. The kind of outdoor lighting you install depends upon the surroundings. A bright urban or suburban setting requires less light than a dark rural one. It's best to illuminate as large an area as possible with a low level of light. Light up large walls, driveways, and paved ground surfaces, creating a background that makes intruders uncomfortable.

There are several kinds of outdoor security lighting systems to consider.

Motion-Sensing Lights

Sensors can be connected to existing lighting or specialized fixtures with built-in sensors can be installed. When a person passes near it, his motion activates the light. The beauty of these devices is they come on only when needed, and they make an intruder think someone in the house has spotted him and switched on the light. This is much better than leaving your porch light on twenty-four hours a day. To most burglars, a lighted porch in

the daytime is like a neon sign announcing, "The residents are out." Keep your security lighting out of reach and protect it from breakage.

Automatic Outdoor Lighting

Lighting can also be controlled by a photo-sensitive switch. When the sun begins to rise in the morning, the light switches off; when daylight gets dim, a photo sensor switches it on. One drawback of the photo sensor is that it can't distinguish between a cloudy, rainy day, and sunset. That means your outdoor lighting could come on during the middle of a dreary day. However, you can install a wall switch to override the sensor signal.

Fixture Placement

Outside the house, you should have two light fixtures on each side of the front door. That way, if the bulb in one burns out, you'll still have a front light on. Install sufficient post lights to ensure that your walkways, fence gates, driveway entrances, and steps have adequate illumination.

Indoor lighting is important, too, especially when you're not a home. The best deterrent is to put lights or TVs on timers in several rooms of the house. Simple, plug-in timers are inexpensive, and you can use them effectively to simulate an occupied house. When you're away, set the timers to go on and off at various

Most sensor-activated lights can be adjusted to prevent nuisance tripping by passing cars or swaying tree branches. Keep yours properly adjusted so it will only turn on the lights when a person enters the area.

How to Install a Motion Sensor on an Existing Light

You can retrofit existing garage and yard lights with motion sensors, increasing the light's effectiveness as a deterrent. The sensors are inexpensive and easy to install with basic tools.

Remove the lightbulb and mount the sensor unit below the light fixture with screws.

Screw the socket adapter into the bulb socket. Screw the lightbulb into the adapter.

Connect the socket adapter to the sensor unit. Test and adjust the sensor as directed by the manufacturer.

intervals. For example, you might have a kitchen light come on early in the evening, then the TV in the family room an hour or two later, and finally a couple of lights in the bedroom.

Secure the Perimeter

A yard with smart perimeter protection may discourage a burglar from approaching. The further out you can keep an intruder, the more visible he or she will be to passersby.

Good perimeter protection begins with a relatively accessible view of your house from the street and from neighboring houses. That doesn't mean you need to go out and chop down your favorite old oak tree; some well-planned pruning may be all it takes.

To begin, take a nighttime walk around the house. Notice which entrances are shrouded from sight by trees or shrubs and which areas would provide excellent protection for a burglar. Once you've determined your problems, prune away.

Trim tree branches up to six feet off the ground to remove hiding places. Keep bushes and hedges trimmed down to near the three-foot level. A low, living wall provides a psychological barrier, even if it doesn't physically exclude anyone from entering the property.

Make sure no climbable trees provide easy access to a second-floor window. Cut away any strong branches close to the house.

The best perimeter protection is a fenced-in yard with lockable gates.

Though expensive, decorative wrought iron is the best type of security fence. It provides no place for a criminal to hide, as a wooden fence does, and is difficult to climb, unlike a chain link fence.

Maintain Your Privacy

Burglars and other criminals like people who give away a lot of information, from address to marital status to vacation habits. Don't be one of those people. Don't put your name on the mailbox. Draw your blinds at night to prevent burglars from "casing" what you have. If you're selling something in a newspaper or online classified ad, don't publish your address. Don't let mail or newspapers pile up when you're away from home. Invest in a shredder and shred all bills, financial documents, and credit card offers before you throw them out. You don't need to live like a hermit; just take care not to broadcast personal information to criminals.

Physical Security

The second line of defense comes from the actual physical devices that prevent unauthorized access should a burglar get near your house. In deciding what level of security you want for your house, consider the crime level in your neighborhood and how much you are willing to spend.

You can purchase everything from bars for the windows to infrared detectors to remotely managed alarm systems with sophisticated sensor technology. However far you choose to go down the road to ultrasophisticated electronic security, good physical measures should be your first priority.

Doors

Good physical security begins with strong doors and quality hardware. Buy the best you can afford. Steel and solid brass are stronger than alloys and plastic. Hollow-core doors provide little security, no matter what type of lock you put on them. Look for metal or solid-core wood doors, at least 1¾ inches thick. Fit the door tightly in its frame with no more than ⅛ inch of clearance between door and frame. If there is an unacceptable gap, consider getting a new door.

Doors with glass panels are like windows—very inviting for a would-be thief who knows that it takes only a few seconds to break the glass and undo the lock. Either replace the door with a solid-core windowless one, install a decorative grille over the glass, or install a nonbreakable plastic overlay. Be sure to use special nonremovable screws.

Hinges

Most front door hinges are on the inside, safe from a burglar's tools. But if your door swings out, hinges and pins are easily removed, exposing the door latch. Once that's accomplished, a burglar just lifts the door out of the frame. If this is the case at your house, replace standard hinge pins with nonremovable ones.

A common weak point in hinges is the

This cutaway photo shows a 3-inch screw penetrating both the doorframe and the adjacent wall stud. This is the best door security you can buy for less than a dollar.

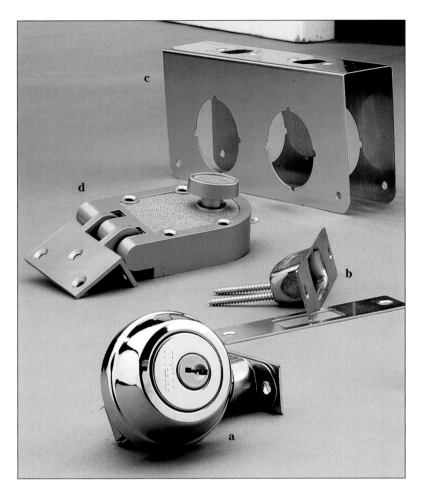

Dead Bolt

The best protection is a dead-bolt lock—separate from the lock on the doorknob—on every entrance door, including the garage. When you turn the key, the lock mechanism slides a strong metal bolt from the door into a metal box (called a strike plate) on the frame. The bolt should project an inch or more into the strike plate.

A tubular dead bolt slides horizontally into the door when you turn a key outside or a thumb knob inside. A double-cylinder dead bolt works only with a key, both inside and out. While providing more security, the risk of not escaping during a fire increases. You must remember to keep the inside key near the lock when you're home, but not close enough that it can be reached through a glass panel. In an emergency, you'll need to use the key to get out of the house.

Interconnected locksets or double-security locksets combine the spring latch and double-cylinder dead bolt. With this setup, a full turn of the inside knob retracts both the latch and the bolt to allow for quick emergency exits.

Rim lock

The rim lock is mounted on the inside of the door near its edge (the rim). A locking device on the door fits into a

Every exterior door should have at least one dead-bolt lock (a). Reinforce bolts and latches with reinforcing plates (b) and boxes (c). Add a rim lock (d) for pick-proof ultimate security.

length of the screws used to attach them. Often, these screws only penetrate the doorframe, not the surrounding wall framing, leaving the door vulnerable to kick-ins. Replacing the hinge screws with 3-inch-long screws will strengthen the door considerably.

Key-in-Nob Lock

The most common door lock has doorknobs inside and out, with a small lock cylinder in the outside knob into which a key is inserted. It's an inexpensive lock with a big drawback: It's the easiest to break. All a thief needs is a heavy object to break off the entire outer knob and lock, exposing the inner mechanism, which can then be easily unlocked. No exterior door should rely entirely on such a lock.

Reinforcing Lock Bolts & Latches

If a door is beginning to show wear around the bolt and latch, it's a good idea to reinforce those areas. Metal reinforcing plates are available to match the rest of the hardware.

plate on the frame. When you turn the key, strong metal bars join the two parts of the lock, much like a hinge pin holds two leaves of a hinge together. Most rim locks mount with ordinary wood screws, which can be torn out easily. Replace them with extra-long screws for the lock and strike plate.

Padlock

Padlocks are typically used for garages, sheds, and workshops. A good, sturdy padlock won't release the key until the padlock is locked. Look for one that is in a rugged laminated case with a ⅜-inch shackle that can resist smashing. There are also double-locking designs that can prevent the shackle from being pried away from its case. No matter what type of padlock you purchase, it will only be as strong as the hasp it's mounted on. The hasp should be secured with bolts mounted on a metal plate and concealed when the padlock is in place.

Patio Doors

Sliding glass patio doors have latches, not locks. Most of the latch systems that come with them provide feeble protection, so most burglars will head straight for a patio door if given a chance. At a minimum, add a security bar, also called a Charlie Bar, that adjusts to fit into the door's bottom track, blocking it from sliding open.

It is also possible for an intruder to lift a sliding glass door off its track. Foil that plan by adjusting the rollers so the door can't be pushed up far enough. You can also insert screws along the upper track of the door, leaving enough room for the door to slide but not enough space to lift out the door.

Windows

Most people fail to secure their windows, providing an open invitation to a burglar. People assume that windows can't be made secure since an intruder could always break the glass. This is a misconception. Most burglars are unwilling to risk attention by breaking glass to gain entry. Making sure the windows can't be silently opened from the outside provides considerable security. Secondary blocking devices should be added to all operable windows. Double-hung windows can be secured with keyed locks and casement windows can be outfitted with lockable cranks.

Keyed Sash Lock

A short aluminum bar at the bottom of the upper sash keeps the bottom sash from moving. A small, keyed lock cylinder holds the bar in place. You'll need to keep the keys away from the windows; make sure everyone in the family knows where to find them in case of emergency.

To prevent intruders from lifting patio doors out of their tracks, drive pan-head screws into the upper track at 8-inch intervals. Drive just deep enough so the door clears the screw heads.

Add extra security to double-hung windows by connecting the sashes with eyebolts. With the window closed, drill ¼-inch holes through the top rail of the inner sash into the bottom rail of the outer sash (take care not to drill all the way through the outer sash). Push ¼-inch × 3-inch eyebolts into the holes to lock the window closed.

Don't Create Another Hazard

- Don't protect against one hazard only to create another,
- Key-operated dead bolts provide good protection only if everyone in the house knows where the keys are.
- Lock bars on sliding patio doors are wise if they can be removed quickly from inside.

Simple Safety Measures

- Do not give out information to strangers over the phone. Instruct children to not let a caller know they're home alone.
- Enforce strict rules about who is allowed through the front door. Any stranger—and that includes a police officer—should provide proper identification.
- Make sure your house numbers are clearly visible from the street day and night. Use six-inch-high numbers made of reflective materials, or use black numbers against a white background. Avoid script letters; they're hard to read. If your house is set back from the road, put the numbers at the driveway entrance. If you live on a corner, be sure the numbers face the street listed as your address.
- If you're ever mentioned in the newspaper, never include your address. Don't include your address in a classified ad.
- Store money, jewelry, and credit cards in a safe place—not in the master bedroom. For jewelry, use a home safe, a vault, or a safety-deposit box.
- Carry the proper amount and type of homeowner's insurance.

Bars

If you live in an especially vulnerable area, consider installing bars on street-level windows. Make sure they have a quick-release feature for emergency exits.

Electronic Security

Electronic security systems can be simple or complex, wired or wireless, inexpensive or costly. But nothing brings 100 percent security. Remotely monitored alarm response times are too slow for the crack burglar. Before a security company contacts the police department and the dispatcher gets a patrol car to your house, enough time may have elapsed for the burglar to get in, take what he or she wants, and leave. Electronic systems are also expensive. A security contract for your house adds another monthly expense. Central-monitored house systems rely on telephone lines for communication. If phone lines are cut, the system can't report burglary or fire but can still sound an alarm that your neighbors may hear.

Protection from Internet Predators

Unfortunately, modern technology has created new frontier in home security: the Internet. Children are regularly sexually solicited online, according to the National Center for Missing and Exploited Children. The convenience of wireless networking also comes with several potential hazards. Privacy and financial records can be stolen over insecure home wireless networks.

Predators reach children through various ways—email, Web sites, chat rooms, instant messages, Usenet newsgroups, peer-to-peer connections—either by establishing a friendly, comfortable one-on-one relationship, or providing immediate access to unsafe content. Children can be indirectly victimized through inappropriate content they see, either out of inadvertent curiosity or from disguised Web addresses, or chat rooms that enable instant messaging.

One of the best ways to keep kids safe is to place computers in common areas, like the family room. If kids know other people are around, they're less likely to be tempted into going to dangerous or inappropriate Web sites.

Another important part of any strategy to protect children from online predators is to make good use of the technology offered through your Internet Service Provider (ISP), including software programs that block content, and filters for search engines that eliminate inappropriate search results. You can also buy inexpensive software that monitors and filters Internet activity.

If you have a wireless network in your home, be sure you have a firewall and that you understand how it works. If you're unsure about your network's security, ask your service provider or call in a professional. If you shop or bank online, the stakes are too high to leave anything to chance.

A Healthy Home Has...

- An exterior that discourages intruders and gives them no hiding places.

- Lights that are triggered by motion or body heat, and timed lights that make the house appear occupied even when it's not.

- Excellent physical security, including solid doors hung on secure hinges and secured with high-quality locks, and windows that lock in place.

- Secure and safe Internet and wireless systems.

SAFE, HEALTHY REMODELING

Have you heard the story about the do-it-yourselfer who carefully isolated his work site, hanging heavy plastic sheeting over every opening, meticulously taping the seams, only to have bushels of fine dust and lead-laden debris blown into every corner of his house when he turned on the heat? He had forgotten to cover the vents!

Don't let this or something similar happen to you. Protect your health and the health of your family by educating yourself about the hazards and pitfalls inherent in any remodeling project.

Just because you're working with a contractor doesn't mean you should relinquish control over your project. It's critical to make sure your contractors are maintaining the same standards as you would if you were doing the work yourself.

Before you begin any remodeling, large or small, remember these simple rules:

- Good timing is first priority. Ventilation is crucial to healthy remodeling. Don't undertake a renovation at a time when you don't want to open windows and doors and install exhaust fans. Sometimes this means forgoing remodeling during winter months in a northern climate or during the summer in a southern environment.

- Select a reputable builder. This is probably the most important remodeling decision you'll make. Look for someone who is willing to take extra steps to protect your indoor environment, someone with interest and experience in healthy building, who has a certification in green building, or who has taken classes and read books on the subject. If you feel like a contractor doesn't share your commitment to healthy building, move on.

- Check references, and visit a project the builder is currently working on (see pages 160 to 166 for information about finding a contractor). Pay attention to how organized the work site is. Some builders never clean up, for example, or only clean up when they can't find their tools. Others systematically clean up every evening before they leave. An orderly work site is a good sign.

Understand what to expect before, during, and after construction. Adopt a remodeling plan that will avoid unhealthy situations or, at least, deal with them should you encounter some. Think through an alternative plan that you can quickly adopt should your family need to leave the house for a day, a night, or even a few weeks.

If you're undertaking a major makeover, plan to live elsewhere, if possible, while the most intense work is going on. This is an especially good idea if you have small children for whom established routines are important. Though living in the basement for a month sounds like a great cost-saving measure, it may be the most expensive decision you make—and not just psychologically. Builders prefer that homeowners leave the house. Work proceeds more rapidly and efficiently when the site is clean, neat, uncluttered, organized, and well ventilated.

A Healthy Approach to a Major Remodel

Building an addition, remodeling a kitchen, and converting a basement or attic to livable space are all major remodeling tasks that can have serious health consequences if not approached systematically.

Before You Begin

A successful healthy remodel begins well before the tools come out. Follow these guidelines.

Evaluate the Building's Condition

Walk through the house with your builder and an environmental inspector. Both are necessary because each looks for different things. A builder will take note of any leaks and dry rot, places where pressure-treated wood has been used, and any problems with the electrical and plumbing systems. The inspector will look for moisture, leaks, asbestos, lead paint, mold, radon, and other environmental hazards that might be exacerbated by the remodeling work. Such an evaluation gives you a

Protect Yourself with Insurance

In order to adequately cover any potential accidents on the work site, your contractor should have public liability insurance, property damage insurance, and workers' compensation for employees and subcontractors. Ask for a certificate of insurance to prove coverage. Call the insurance carrier and ask if the coverage is still in effect and whether it will remain so during the expected length of your project.

In addition, ask your contractor to provide a written warranty on all labor and materials (in addition to manufacturers' warranties) for a period of at least one year. Make sure it includes consequential damage, such as discoloration to a floor due to a leaky skylight that he or she installed. Even if your contractor is known as someone who "stands behind the job," an explicit warranty clarifies exactly what to expect if problems arise.

A specific warranty should be included in all copies of the contract, and it should be signed by someone with the authority to speak for the company.

good starting point for establishing remodeling procedures based on all of the conditions found. Be aware that hazardous materials require special removal methods and that the work should always be done by certified contractors. After the inspector and contractor have identified all the requirements and potential problems of the project, you'll be able to proceed with planning and building with no nasty surprises.

To find an indoor air-quality or environmental inspector, look in the telephone book under "Air-quality measuring service" or "Building inspection—environmental." Or call the EPA or your local or state health department.

Prepare Drawings & Specifications

Make sure your plan drawings include the whole house, not just the part you're working on. Think of your house as an interconnected system. Changes to one part could very well affect another. One part often adversely affected is the heating and ventilation systems. Make sure your drawings include new and existing ductwork, so you'll know where the air comes from and where it is going.

Insist on taking an active role in specifying materials for the construction. Select all materials carefully. Work with your architect and/or contractor to be certain materials are up to your standard of what is healthy and what is not. If you or anyone in your family has chemical sensitivities, you'll want to test questionable materials with the aid of a medical doctor to make certain you don't choose materials that cause a reaction. If you simply want materials that don't offgas or otherwise injure physical health, the

Building Materials chapter (see pages 46 to 59) is a good guide. By choosing an architect and/or contractor with experience in healthy and/or green building (see pages 160 to 166), you'll have a knowledgeable advocate with your interests in mind.

Obtain Materials Safety Data Sheets (MSDS), available from manufacturers and retailers, which list ingredients of products and provide the necessary practical information on their safe use. If you don't understand the sheet, ask your environmental inspector to interpret it for you.

Prepare Yourself Emotionally

Remodeling inevitably takes longer and costs more than you anticipate. Living in a half-finished, torn-up house is like living on the edge of a demilitarized zone. Workmen don't show up when they're supposed to; products don't arrive on time; and when they do, they may be the wrong size or color. The whole process can be a huge emotional strain, especially when two people are making decisions together. Don't let the stress get you down. Nurture family relationships throughout the project. Relax, and do your best to enjoy this worthwhile adventure. If your remodeling project is particularly extensive, take the time to set up one room as a remodeling-free zone. No work should be done in this room; no materials stored there. Ideally, it should be fairly isolated from the construction noise. This is the place you can seek refuge when everywhere else in the house is caught up in the remodeling whirlwind.

Prepare Your Materials

Make sure your contractor or you your-

Let the Buyer Beware.

If you are particularly concerned about any specific building product, ask your contractor, the dealer, or salesperson what's in it before you purchase or approve it. You can also try calling the manufacturer or the EPA for more information about a particular product and whether it is known to have any adverse effect on individuals or the environment. All manufacturers are required to provide a MSDS for their building products upon request, and many have the MSDS available online.

Persistent requests for information worked with the paint industry. Fifteen years ago, only a limited group of specialty manufacturers produced low-VOC paints. When Glidden introduced a line of zero-VOC paints in 1993, the company met with instant success. All major paint manufacturers have followed suit. Now, most U.S. paint manufacturers market zero- or low-VOC paint.

You have a right to know what is in the air you breathe. Eventually, a few years from now, laws will be passed regulating toxic ingredients in building products, but we can't rely on that now. It's still let the buyer beware.

---

self are doing the prep work necessary to make potentially unhealthy materials as safe as possible.

If, for instance, you purchase composite-wood products, make sure they are stored outside and are sealed adequately prior to installation. The same is true for new carpeting. If possible, unroll the carpet in a covered outdoor area or warehouse, and allow it to air out for several weeks prior to installation. Such precautions reduce the initial introduction of VOCs into your home, so you'll be on top of the health curve from the onset.

To make certain the builder does not introduce harmful toxins to the work site, write up a list of general requirements and post them at several highly visible locations on the site.

Prepare the Work Site

Isolate the work site from the rest of the house by hanging plastic sheeting (6 to 12 mil polyethylene) over interior doorways, sealing it on the top and down both sides with tape. For additional protection, hang two sheets. If the interior doorway must be used during construction, overlap the two sheets, but leave one side of each unattached on opposite sides. To use the doorway, weave your way between the sheets. Don't forget to seal any exposed ductwork, grills, and return vents. Once pollutants are spread around the duct system, they are difficult or impossible to clean.

Hang a fire extinguisher (Type ABC) close by, in case of emergency. And, if there's a chance nails may litter the work site, driveway, or yard, make sure everyone in the family has been immunized against tetanus, and caution them to wear shoes at all times.

Designate an area (ideally well outside the building envelope) for tasks like sawing and sanding lumber in order to minimize the amount of sawdust in the house. This is particularly important if there will be any pressure-treated lumber in the project.

SAFE, HEALTHY REMODELING

painting—whenever work is going on. The fan may get pretty grungy, but it will still work. For large areas or very dirty operations, bring in more fans.

Know When to Leave

Not all remodelings foul indoor air so badly that you need to vacate the house. However, to keep you and your family healthy, pay attention to your sense of smell. If something is clouding the air or causing an odor (such as offgassing from newly applied polyurethane on hardwood floors), it may be time to pack a suitcase and leave the house. If work will stop while you're gone, open windows, and cleanse the house with air while you're gone. Don't second guess yourself if you're particularly sensitive to chemicals.

Demolition

Some remodeling projects involve a significant amount of demolition. This phase is an important one because you may encounter nasty materials that need special care in order not to be dispersed throughout the house and cause indoor air quality problems later on.

Micro-organisms

Wear a respirator when removing molds. This is a good day for homeowners to vacate the house. If you find evidence of animals, birds, or insects, take care not to spread contamination. Dampen it down if you can, then (wearing a mask) carefully shovel it into a waste container. Avoid making a dust cloud. Clean up the residue with a vacuum that has a HEPA filter. Be sure to seek expert advice when large amounts are found.

Asbestos

The EPA suggests you hire a certified

Use sheets of polyethylene to seal off the work area. Make sure a fire extinguisher is located on the work site, and post your healthy remodeling rules where all can see them.

Ventilate! Ventilate! Ventilate!

Provide lots of ventilation to remove pollutants as they're being generated. The best way is by creating negative air pressure so air flows from the occupied space, through the work site, and out the window. Invest in a 20-inch, 3000-cfm window fan and install it in a window (preferably where it doesn't blow into your neighbor's house), set on high, blowing out. Bring in replacement air by opening two or three additional windows on the opposite wall.

Maintain air-pressure control throughout the entire project—during demolition, sanding, cutting, drywall sanding, professional to identify and remove all friable or soft asbestos. Some very hard materials, such as floor tiles and siding, may be safe for homeowners to remove, provided you carefully follow EPA guidelines.

Lead

It's best to hire a certified professional to remove lead paint. Keep children, pregnant women, and pets away while work is going on. Never sand lead paint or use a heat gun to remove it. If you elect to remove materials containing lead yourself, wear a cartridge respirator face mask certified for lead removal.

Insulation

Be extremely careful with fiberglass insulation. It should not be handled without gloves and respiratory protection. When demolishing a wall containing fiberglass, rock wool, or cellulose, wear a mask and good quality skin protection. Avoid creating dust clouds. Ventilate!

Wood Dust

Wear eye protection and a particle mask anytime you're sanding wood. When working with pressure-treated and engineered wood, wear a mask approved for dust and organic vapors, and ventilate the area. Dispose of scrap immediately and do not burn. Gypsum board can be even more noxious when sanded or sawed; wear a good dust mask and ventilate.

If You're Doing the Work Yourself…

Safety while the work is ongoing is just as important as long-term building health. Most renovation-related injuries are caused by falls, lifting, and careless use of tools and materials. If you are doing some or all of the work yourself, make safety a top priority. Keep a tidy work site. Don't work when fatigued. Use products according to their labels.

If you're a do-it-yourselfer and you're concerned about healthy building, the most important tool you purchase may be your personal ventilator or respirator. Use ventilators or respirators whenever you're working with hazardous materials. Take care to choose the appropriate filters for the job. While a cotton face mask (the kind with two rubber bands, about $10 for a package of 50 at your local hardware store) does an okay job filtering out large particles, it should only be used outdoors and is worthless with gas and vapors. For maximum protection, you need a half-face air purifying respirator covering the nose and mouth.

Air-purifying respirators contain a filter that removes specific air contaminants. Different filters, cartridges, and canisters are designed to filter out specific pollutants, so you must first identify the air contaminant you're working with. Read the manufacturer's instructions for cartridge maintenance and replacement, or consult the Occupational Safety and Health Administration (OSHA) Web site (see page 171), which can help you select an appropriate respirator, calculate your exposure assessment, and establish a cartridge-changing schedule.

Respirators cost from $20 to $50; filters cost anywhere from $18 (package of 20) for dust and up to $12 (package of two) for organic vapors, paint, and pesticides. Quality respirators, masks, and filters are available at most large hardware or home stores. They are conveniently labeled for the type of contaminants they're designed to remove. Select a respirator approved by the National Institute for Occupational Safety and Health (NIOSH).

Many gases and chemicals are also absorbed through the skin, so it's best to cover up your body as much as possible. Skin contributes significantly to overall exposure and includes mucous membranes and the eyes, either by contact with vapors or by direct skin contact with the substance. Although wearing a long sleeve shirt and pants, in addition to a proper mask, is a wise decision, don't forget to remove your clothes once exposed to chemicals and launder them as soon as possible. When the day's work is done, a shower and a change of clothes will be more than refreshing; it can be the difference between waking up the next morning refreshed and ready to go or waking up the next morning feeling congested, itchy, and generally sick.

Gases

When dealing with products that give off odors or vapors (paints, solvents, varnishes, glues), remove all porous materials—stuffed furniture, draperies, carpeting, rugs, etc.—from the project area. Such porous materials absorb gases and vapors, then release them slowly over time long after your project is completed.

After the Work Is Done

Just because the construction work is done, doesn't mean you should let your guard down. Materials continue to offgas long after the hammering and sawing have stopped.

Keep ventilation fans moving during cleaning, sanding, and finishing, so volatile gases from paints and finishes are dumped out of the house, rather than soaked up by interior materials (wood, drywall, upholstery, carpeting). Don't remove any of the plastic from the vents or turn on the heating system until all work is finished, cleanup is completed, and all of the paint has thoroughly dried. Continue to operate ventilation fans for a couple of days after work is finished, or until there is no easily detectable odor.

Masks & Respirators

Protection for your lungs is as critical as protection for your eyes and ears. There are four basic kinds of masks and respirators.

Cotton facemasks don't fit tightly on the face so they are, at best, a cheaper but less effective alternative to a particulate respirator. Use only for sanding, sawing, and cutting outdoors. They offer no protection against gases and vapors.

A particulate respirator protects against inhalation of dust and mist. These do not remove vapors. Use for any job that generates particulates, such as sanding, cutting sheetrock or plywood. Conduct sanding and sawing activities outdoors.

Cartridge, or canister, respirators use a medium such as activated charcoal to remove dangerous gases and vapors from the air. They do not protect against airborne particles. Use for such projects as painting, staining wood, applying conventional caulk—whenever you're working with a substance that has a strong odor. If you can smell it, your body is capable of absorbing it through your nose and skin.

Combination respirators have filters for both particulates and vapors. Use when working with materials such as conventional fiberglass insulation where the main concern is to protect against inhaling small glass fibers, yet formaldehyde-based adhesives are used to bind the fibers together. The only downside to this type of filter is they are often heavy and slightly cumbersome.

HIRING HEALTH-CONSCIOUS CONTRACTORS

Whether building a new house from the ground up or adding a room onto your existing home, the main difference between a health-conscious construction project and one using conventional materials and methods is that the "healthy" option requires more attention. In the case of people with known chemical sensitivities, the process requires much more attention.

For best results, the whole team—homeowner, architect, contractor, any engineers or specialists—needs to get together early and work collaboratively throughout the entire process, brainstorming solutions to problems, agreeing on design, specifying materials, and avoiding potential pitfalls. To avoid difficulties, communication is key, so be prepared to take an active role.

In order to communicate clearly, first decide why you want to incorporate healthy building into your project in the first place. The answer to this question will help guide your decisions.

- Are you or is a member of your family chemically sensitive?
- Are you as concerned about the environment as you are about your family's health?
- Do you have small children in your household?
- Does any member of your household have allergies, asthma, or recurrent respiratory problems?
- Is anyone chronically ill?

Become Part of the Healthy Building Community

To build a healthy house, you almost need to become an expert on healthy building. Fortunately, this isn't as hard as it sounds. Begin by becoming familiar with the concepts involved in a healthy home (you're already doing that by reading this book). Make a habit of reading publications that cover healthy building topics. Go to home shows. The Web is a handy resource tool. Many homeowners document their building and remodeling projects in personal Web logs ("blogs") and on Web sites. These are great resources for firsthand information on how products and techniques work in the field. Clip articles; bookmark favorite Web sites; and create files of the materials, technologies, and resources you want to use. The more information you can show your team, the more quickly they can tune into what you want and expect.

Try to obtain a green/healthy checklist of materials and building techniques to help you design and build your dream home/addition. Ask your architect and/or builder if they have put together such a checklist or if they can recommend software that incorporates healthy floor plans and specifications. Some contractors maintain such a checklist and use a rating system to gauge how healthy or green the final product will be. A rating of five, for example, is top notch, where a rating of two is above standard. Because

several problems are site or region specific, your local builders' association may already have a checklist designed for your area.

If chemical sensitivities are a problem, you'll need to test various materials, especially those on the interior such as paints, varnishes, flooring, wood trim, etc. It helps to know what you're talking about. Working closely with your doctor, ask your builder to gather samples of materials suspected of causing sensitivity problems. Usually, doctors recommend that samples be isolated in a plastic bag and brought to their office where, under medical supervision, the person with chemically sensitivities is introduced to small amounts of suspect materials, then monitored to see if these materials cause a reaction.

You may want to branch out into the green building network to get a house that is environmentally sound as well as personally healthy. Several types of green building software exist. One, the "Green Building Advisor" (published by Building Green, Inc.), is a brainstorming tool for anyone wanting to reduce the environmental impact of a particular building or

Costs

Healthy building costs should not exceed 1 to 3 percent more than standard construction costs, if at all. Many green building techniques actually reduce construction costs, and many aspects of healthy building cost little or nothing to implement. What little additional cost there is can usually be attributed to your contractor's learning curve, or labor costs. A smaller percentage is due to materials expense. As demand and availability grows, these prices will become equivalent to conventional materials. If your estimates are coming in too high, this may be an indicator that your contractor is not as familiar with the materials as you may like him or her to be. Keep in mind, when it comes time to sell your home, real estate analysts estimate the resale value of healthy homes to be 5 percent to 15 percent greater than conventionally-built homes, making it a wise financial investment.

renovation project. It's easy to use. You simply enter information and the software generates a list of strategies relevant to the project, organized into categories for easy review. It also includes overview information on green building design, an extensive green products database, and a resource guide. Such software can save you hours of research. Look for an architect or builder who already has such software or is willing to purchase it.

Whatever your project, you'll need to communicate your wishes to your architect and or contractor.

Finding the Right Professionals

Remember, by being in the market for a health-conscious builder/architect, you're a pioneer in the field, searching for other pioneers. Finding an architect or builder familiar with healthy construction isn't easy, but they are out there, and their numbers are increasing every day.

Start your search by driving around your neighborhood. Most contractors post signs at job sites. Knock on the door and speak with the homeowner. Visiting actual remodels is a great source of design ideas.

Ask your friends, and friends of friends. Have any of them had experience with healthy building? Be bold! The more people you ask, the more useful names you'll gather.

Tap into the local design community. Check the Yellow Pages to see if any interior decorators or designers claim special expertise in green or healthy design.

Go on home tours, subscribe to regional home design magazines, read the home and business sections of your local newspaper. The bigger the city, the more options you'll have to choose from. You'll find that a few firms specialize in green building. Others may have a specialty in health-conscious design, or natural building, energy efficiency, or accessibility. Seek out a professional with experience in the areas you want to incorporate into your project.

Oftentimes, when you find one piece of the puzzle—an architect, general contractor, or home builder—the rest of the pieces rapidly fall into place. If you find a suitable architect, he or she will likely know of a compatible builder who will have a list of reliable tradespeople and so on.

If local sources don't turn up a suitable builder, check out the following.

- Contact your city or county to find out about city- or county-sponsored healthy building programs and related incentives.
- Look for local healthy-building non-profit organizations, or locate a local chapter of a national organization dedicated to green and healthy building (such as the local chapter of the American Lung Association).
- The National Association of the Remodeling Industry (NARI) now has a certified green builder training program, and can help locate a contractor in your area.
- The National Association of Home Builders (NAHB) can provide a list of members in your area.
- Look for local members of the United States Green Building Council (USGBC).
- Get a copy of *Green Spec*, a book detailing specifications for building green.

Interviewing Architects, Builders, & General Contractors

It's always a good idea to chat with a contractor or tradesperson you might be working with, but it is absolutely essential for any sort of healthy remodeling project. You'll be working closely with your architect and contractors, so it's important that you have a comfortable rapport and that they take you and your commitment to healthy building seriously. Don't be afraid to ask any question that might occur to you. Smart contractors always appreciate savvy consumers because such customers always say what they want and appreciate good work. Any potential contractor who's turned off by your questioning isn't worth considering anyway.

Ask open-ended questions when interviewing to elicit the most valuable information. For example, instead of asking a contractor, "Do you follow construction practices that minimize contamination and protect indoor air quality?" Pose the question in this manner, "What construction techniques do you employ in order to minimize contamination and protect indoor air quality?" Answering the latter question actually requires a little knowledge!

Have a list of questions on hand whenever you interview potential contractors. Here are some questions you may want to ask your potential contractor.

- "Is healthy building important to you? Why?" You know you have a dedicated professional when the answer deals with quality, durable, sustainable construction, reduced environmental impact, less maintenance, and a concern for human health as well as the health of the planet.

- "Are green/healthy specifications part of your basic contract?" A dedicated professional won't list healthy specifications as options; they will be built into the basic contract.

- "Have you purchased green/healthy products and know how to work with their variable availability and lead times?"

- "What is your strategy for reducing interior pollutants?" Listen for answers like "taping off duct work."

- "Which healthy products have you used before?" Listen for answers including low-VOC paints, sealants, caulking, stains, and formaldehyde-free particleboard and insulation.

- "What practices do you employ to prevent mold from growing in your houses?" Answers should include keeping building materials dry; flashing around wall openings and other techniques to keep rainwater out of walls; and ensuring good interior ventilation, particularly in the bathrooms and kitchen.

After you've interviewed a candidate, ask yourself these questions. Don't make a choice until you're satisfied with the answer to each.

- Does this person understand how building practices relate to the broader environment? Is this person giving you the "right" answers just to get your business, or does he or she demonstrate real commitment to health? Can this builder show any proof of that?

- Does this person demonstrate a general knowledge of healthy building? If you get a blank stare when asking questions about low-VOC paints, formaldehyde-free insulation, sealed-combustion appliances, or alternatives to composite-wood products, chances are this person is not familiar with healthy construction.

- Does this person have hands-on experience with healthy building? Can he or she point to specific projects in his or her portfolio and provide references and phone numbers? Is this builder glad to have you call on former clients and visit completed projects?

- If you are interested in an unconventional material or technique, is this person willing to get the information you want? If no one in the area has done what you want, can this person accomplish something out of the ordinary?

- Does this person keep up with advances in the field of healthy construction? Is this person a member of any green/healthy design organizations and has he or she participated in any building seminars and conferences to receive up-to-date information? Does this person read major publications, such as *Environmental Building News?*

- Does this builder understand the importance of a team approach in pro-

ducing a good, healthy home? Does he or she see the architect, the subcontractors, and you, the client, as equally important players on the same team, working together to create a high-quality home where you and your family can be happy and comfortable?

- Is this architect or builder knowledgeable and enthusiastic about healthy building, or does he or she sound unenthusiastic about the prospect of a long-term project with extensive homeowner involvement?

- Does the builder understand that it may be difficult to obtain some important materials, and that longer lead times are required in a green/healthy building project? Does he or she plan to deliver comparable quality as is expected with conventional products?

- Do you like this person? Do all parties communicate well? Do you feel like this person takes you seriously? Are your wishes, ideas, and requirements being heard?

In addition to doing your healthy-home due diligence, there are several common-sense steps you should take. Before hiring either an architect or contractor, always check references. When hiring a contractor, solicit bids from several different people. Ask to see a copy of the contractor's certificate of insurance or the name of his or her insurance agency to verify worker's compensation, property damage, and personal liability coverage, so you'll be protected if injuries or damage occurs.

When you've made a selection, make sure you get a detailed, written contract specifying total price of the work, payment schedule, provision for changes,

Rules for
the Site

Making sure your contractor is using healthy materials and techniques is only the first part of the battle. A construction site, no matter how healthy the building materials, can be a very unhealthy place, especially for allergy sufferers or the chemically sensitive, if it isn't kept clean and well ventilated. Work with your contractor before the job begins to lay down some ground rules for a clean and healthy work site, and make sure the contractor passes these rules on to all his or her subcontractors. Here are some good examples.

- Insist that there be no smoking on or near the job site, and require that no gasoline-powered tools be used within the building envelope at any time.
- Clearly define where all debris and scrap should be disposed of. For larger jobs, this means renting a dumpster. All demolition debris and waste should be carried to the dumpster on a predetermined path (not through living spaces). This may require installing a chute for second-story jobs.
- Require that all work areas and ductwork be sealed off with polyethylene sheeting before work begins.
- Insist on a daily cleanup of the job site. Make sure the job site is thoroughly cleaned between stages of construction (such as between wiring and drywall installation) so that debris isn't enclosed in walls or under flooring. Be especially diligent with wood chips and sawdust left after framing and electrical installation. You'd be amazed at the debris drywall contractors and flooring contractors will leave in place. If you are especially sensitive, require that HEPA-filter vacuums be used for cleanup.
- Require that workers use only a bathroom within the job site (if possible) or provide an alternate facility (rent a portable outhouse, if necessary). There's no point in sealing the job site if workers track debris and particles into the house on their way to the bathroom.
- Ask that any new ductwork be stored away from the job site until it is time to install it. This will help prevent construction debris from contaminating the new HVAC system.
- Define in advance where trucks may be parked and tools may be stored.

Once the work has begun, take a few moments every night to inspect the job site. Don't do it while workers are on site, but, after everyone has packed up, check to make sure the guidelines are being followed. If some workers aren't following guidelines, bring it to your contractor's attention immediately.

Building a New Home? Choose a Healthy Site

If you're building a new home from the ground up, you're lucky. You can specify healthy materials and utilities from the onset and incorporate them into your design. You also have the opportunity to choose a healthy site. When looking for possible places to build, consider the following:

A healthy site is:

- Free from air and noise pollution from traffic.
- Away from regular pesticide applications (golf course, vineyard, etc.), but if located nearby, at least upwind from pesticide applications, and never in a valley below, as pesticides are heavier than air and will settle in the lowest area.
- At a distance from high voltage power lines, cellular phone repeaters, and microwave relay stations.
- Has good air circulation—locations on crests have better air quality due to greater air movement.
- Has uncontaminated soils—no previous use of pesticides and herbicides.

detailed list of specifications and materials, starting and completion dates. Make sure you understand the terms before you sign anything.

Specifications & Plans

Architects (and some builders) draw up specifications for each project, a detailed account of materials to be used and techniques of application. Be sure you understand the specs for your project. If it's not sufficiently detailed or if the terminology in a critical area is too general, ask for details. (For example, "paint" is too general; "no-VOC interior paint" is better.) Don't be content with building-trade jargon; ask for product names so you can check a Materials Safety Data Sheet (MSDS). Ask your architect and/or builder to review it with you, and make

sure you understand everything before you approve the document. Keep a copy on file and check it against what's actually on the job site. Specify in writing that you must approve all substitutions. If you need to make a change during the job, put change orders in writing.

Create clear, written instructions for criteria to be considered in any future material selection. Among those instructions, be sure to list that if the general contractor is experiencing difficulty with a product he or she must call you for a reevaluation. If substitutions must be made, require a MSDS and physical samples be submitted to your architect for approval. And make sure you've laid out a process that requires your notification and approval of any material substitutions that may be necessary.

RESOURCES

Healthy Home Update

ORGANIZATIONS & RESOURCES

Environmental Defense

800-591-1919

www.scorecard.org

Enter your zip code and find out what pollutants are being released into your community.

Environmental Health News

www.EnvironmentalHealthNews.org

Daily e-mails of news, reports, scientific discoveries, and links to health in the U.S. and around the world.

Environmental Working Group (EWG)

202-667-6982

www.ewg.org

Source of excellent reports, including "Body Burden: Pollution in People, Not Too Pretty."

BOOKS & MAGAZINES

The Seventh Generation Guide to a Toxin-Free Home, available from Seventh Generation, distributors of healthy, nontoxic household products.

802-658-3773

www.seventhgeneration.com

Prescriptions for a Healthy House by Paula Baker-Laporte, Erica Elliot, and John Banta (New Society Publishers, 2001).

Give Your House a Health Audit

BOOKS & MAGAZINES

Homes That Heal: And Those That Don't by Athena Thompson (New Society Publishers, 2004).

www.homesthatheal.com

Water

ORGANIZATIONS & RESOURCES

Environmental Protection Agency (EPA)
800-426-4791
www.epa.gov/safewater
Get Consumer Confidence Reports (CCRs) and find out where your water comes from and any violations made by the supplier.

The National Sanitation Foundation
800-NSF-MARK
www.nsf.org/certified/DWTU
Find a list of certified water-treatment devices.

PRODUCTS

Gaiam
www.gaiam.com
A good source for water filters.

Lifekind
www.lifekind.com
A good source for shower filters.

Indoor Air

ORGANIZATIONS & RESOURCES

American Lung Association
800-LUNG-USA
www.lungsusa.org

Consumer Product Safety Commission
800-638-CPSC
www.cpsc.gov
Information on products containing asbestos.

Environmental Protection Agency (EPA)
202-272-0167
www.epa.gov/iaq
Resources for mold, lead, asbestos, radon, and other indoor-air-quality problems. For a list of asbestos-abatement contractors in your area:
202-554-1404
800-424-5323 (lead information hotline)

Fragrance Product Information Network
www.fpinva.org
Helpful articles about chemicals in fragrance and how they impact health.

National Radon Hotline
800-767-7236

National Safety Council's Radon Program
800-644-6999

PRODUCTS

Less EMF
888-526-4237
www.lessemf.com
Supplier of gauss meters, microwave oven testers, computer shielding, and more.

BOOKS & MAGAZINES

An Alternative Approach to Allergies by Theron G. Randolph, M.D. and Ralph W. Moss, Ph.D. (Harper & Row, 1990).

Cell Phones: Invisible Hazards in the Wireless Age by Dr. George Carlo and Martin Schram (Carroll and Graf, 2001).

Building Materials
ORGANIZATIONS & RESOURCES
**The Healthy Building Network,
Institute for Self-Reliance**
202-232-4108
www.healthybuilding.net

The Healthy Flooring Network
www.healthyflooring.org

The Home Energy Saver
hes.lbl.gov
An online calculator developed by
Lawrence Berkeley National Laboratory
takes data input by users and reports the
measures that will be effective in reducing
utility bills and environmental impact.

MSDS Solutions
www.msds.com
A source for Material Safety Data Sheets.

PRODUCTS
Antique Drapery Rod Co., Inc.
214-653-1733
www.antiquedraperyrod.com
Supplier of real milk paint.

AFM Safecoat
800-239-0321
www.afmsafecoat.com
Manufacturer of paints, sealers (including
low-VOC sealers), stains, and caulk.

Marmoleum
www.marmoleum.com
Manufacturer of natural linoleum.

BOOKS & MAGAZINES
*Green Building Products: The Green Spec
Guide to Residential Building Materials,*
edited by Alex Wilson and Mark Piepkorn
(New Society Publishers, 2005).

Environmental Building News published
by Building Green
www.buildinggreen.com

Furnishings & Appliances
ORGANIZATIONS & RESOURCES
The Green Guide
www.thegreenguide.com

Greenpeace
*www.greenpeace.org.uk/Products/Toxics/
chemicalhouse.cfm*
A good Web site for locating suitable
furnishings.

PRODUCTS
Casa Natura
505-820-7634
www.casanaturainc.com
Sells a wide range of products and furnishings. Daryl Stanton, the owner, is available for consultations and interior design.

EcoChoices
www.ecochoices.com
Environmental home furnishing.

Earth Weave Carpet Mills
706-278-8200
www.earthweave.com
Natural carpet and floor coverings.

PhoneLabs
212-481-6166
www.phonelabs.com
Makers of the Dock 'n' Talk cell-phone
dock.

Housekeeping
ORGANIZATIONS & RESOURCES
EPA
Glossary of cleaning products and hazards associated with them:
www.epa.gov/grtlakes/seahome/ housewaste/house/products.htm

BOOKS & MAGAZINES
Green Clean by Linda Mason Hunter and Mikki Halpin, (Melcher Media, 2005).
www.greenclean.com

Better Basics for the Home: Simple Solutions for Less Toxic Living by Annie Berthold-Bond (Three Rivers Press, 1999).

The Household Product Management Wheel offers information and tips on thirty-six common household chemical products. To order, contact the Environmental Hazards Management Institute.
603-868-1496
www.ehmi.org

Pests
ORGANIZATIONS & RESOURCES
Environmental Health Coalition
619-235-0281
www.environmentalhealth.org

EPA, Office of Pesticide Programs
703-305-7695
www.epa.gov/pesticides

Beyond Pesticides
The National Coalition Against the Misuse of Pesticides
202-543-5450
www.beyondpesticides.org

National Pesticide Information Center
800-858-7378
npic.orst.edu

Around the Yard
ORGANIZATIONS & RESOURCES
The Healthy Building Network, Institute for Self Reliance
202-232-4108
www.healthybuilding.net
Sells a kit for testing for arsenic in lumber.

Washington Toxics Coalition
www.watoxics.org
Declare your yard a "Pesticide Free Zone." Signs available from the coalition's Web site.

House Systems
ORGANIZATIONS & RESOURCES
Home Ventilating Institute
www.hvi.org
Features a complete listing of ventilating options from many manufacturers.

Sound
PRODUCTS
Franklin International
800-877-4583
www.titebond.com
Manufacturer of Titebond Multipurpose Sealant.

Homasote Company
800-257-9491
www.homasote.com
Manufacturer of sound-reducing wallboard.

Bonded Logic, Inc.
480-812-9114
www.bondedlogic.com
Manufacturer of UltraTouch Natural Fiber
Insulation, made from recycled blue jeans.

Light
ORGANIZATIONS & RESOURCES
Light for Health
800-468-1104
www.lightforhealth.com

PRODUCTS
Velux USA
www.veluxusa.com
Manufacturer of tubular skylights.

Safety
ORGANIZATIONS & RESOURCES
U.S. Fire Administration
301-447-1000
www.usfa.fema.gov
www.usfa.fema.gov/safety/sprinklers/
Information on residential sprinklers.

PRODUCTS
NOFIRE technologies
www.nofiretechnologies.com
Manufacturer of fire-retardant paint.

Chains of Life
www.chainsoflife.com
Manufacturer of fire escape ladders.

Security
BOOKS & MAGAZINES
Do-It-Yourself Extreme Home Security Guide
by David Barbasso, (PublishAmerica,
2005).

Safe, Healthy Remodeling
ORGANIZATIONS & RESOURCES
**Occupational Safety and Health
Administration (OSHA)**
www.osha.gov

BOOKS AND MAGAZINES
*Green Remodeling: Changing the World
One Room at a Time* by David Johnston
and Kim Master (New Society Publishers,
2004).

Healthy Housing Renovation Planner
Order from the Canadian Mortgage and
Housing Corp.
800-668-2642
www.cmhc.ca

Hiring Health-&-Safety Conscious Building Professionals
ORGANIZATIONS & RESOURCES
**The National Association of the
Remodeling Industry (NARI)**
800-611-NARI
www.nari.org
NARI now has a certified green builder
training program and can help locate a
contractor in your area.

**United States Green Building Council
(UGBC)**
202-82-USGBC
www.usgbc.org

BOOKS & MAGAZINES
No Regrets Remodeling by Alex Wilson,
et al., (Home Energy Magazine, 1997).

INDEX

CONTRIBUTORS

Flooring product materials p. 56 contributed by:
Marmoleum by Forbo Linoleum
866-627-6653
www.themarmoleumstore.com

Photos pp. 89 and 96 contributed by:
University of Nebraska Department of Entomology
402-472-8691
http://entomology.unl.edu

Photo p. 127 contributed by:
VELUX-America, Inc.
800-888-3589
www.VELUXusa.com

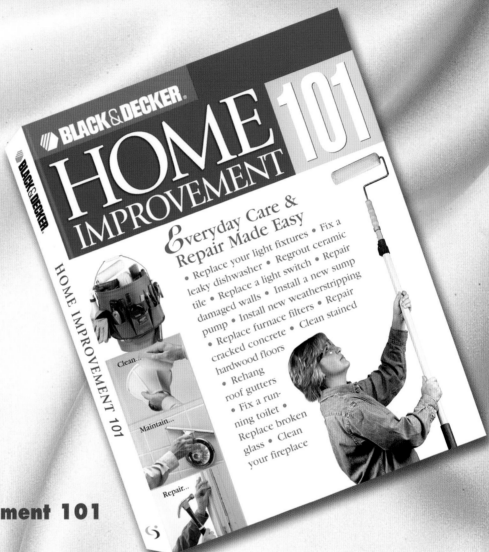

CREATIVE PUBLISHING INTERNATIONAL

IdeaWise Basements & Attics
IdeaWise Bathrooms
IdeaWise Decks & Patios
IdeaWise Garages
IdeaWise Kitchens
IdeaWise Porches & Sunrooms
IdeaWise Storage
IdeaWise Yards & Gardens

ISBN 1-58923-203-8

ISBN 1-58923-204-6

ISBN 0-86573-158-9

ISBN 1-58923-157-0

CREATIVE PUBLISHING INTERNATIONAL

18705 LAKE DRIVE EAST
CHANHASSEN, MN 55317

WWW.CREATIVEPUB.COM